IN THE PRONA

OF THE

TEMPLE OF WISDOM

Containing the history of the true and the false Rosicrucians with an introduction into the mysteries of the hermetic philosophy and an appendix containing the principles of the yoga-philosophy of the Rosicrucians and alchemists.

Franz Hartmann

ISBN 1-56459-219-7

Kessinger Publishing's
Rare Mystical Reprints

THOUSANDS OF SCARCE BOOKS ON THESE AND OTHER SUBJECTS:

Freemasonry * Akashic * Alchemy * Alternative Health * Ancient Civilizations * Anthroposophy * Astrology * Astronomy * Aura * Bible Study * Cabalah * Cartomancy * Chakras * Clairvoyance * Comparative Religions * Divination * Druids * Eastern Thought * Egyptology * Esoterism * Essenes * Etheric * ESP * Gnosticism * Great White Brotherhood * Hermetics * Kabalah * Karma * Knights Templar * Kundalini * Magic * Meditation * Mediumship * Mesmerism * Metaphysics * Mithraism * Mystery Schools * Mysticism * Mythology * Numerology * Occultism * Palmistry * Pantheism * Parapsychology * Philosophy * Prosperity * Psychokinesis * Psychology * Pyramids * Qabalah * Reincarnation * Rosicrucian * Sacred Geometry * Secret Rituals * Secret Societies * Spiritism * Symbolism * Tarot * Telepathy * Theosophy * Transcendentalism * Upanishads * Vedanta * Wisdom * Yoga * *Plus Much More!*

DOWNLOAD A FREE CATALOG AT:
www.kessinger.net

OR EMAIL US AT:
books@kessinger.net

CONTENTS

Chapter One—Introduction. Occult Literature—Allegorical language of the Rosicrucian books—Its secret meaning..................7

Chapter Two—The Hermetic Philosophy. The Neoplatonists—Ammonius Saccas—Plotinus—Malchus Porphyrius—Jamblichus—Proclus—Hierocles..14

Chapter Three—Mediaeval Philosophers. 'Magic," according to Cornelias Agrippa...24

Chapter Four—Among the Adepts. "The Brotherhood of the Golden and Rosy Cross"—Occult and mysterious powers—Adepts and Sages—Alchymists and Goldmakers—The True History of Flamel—The Count de Saint Germain—Cagliostro—The art of making alchemical gold—Well-authenticated facts.................................35

Chapter Five—The Rosicrucian "Orders." "History" of the Rosicrucians—The Universal Reformation; the Fama Fraternitatis and the Confessio—Truth and Fiction—The Chemical Marriage of Christian Rosencruetz—Valentin Andreae—The Sphinx Rosaceae—Andreas von Carolstadt—Theophrastus Paracelsus—Rosicrucian Literature......49

Chapter Six—Pseudo Rosicrucians. Imposters and Fools. Mysticism during the Middle Ages—Secret Societies—Schroepfer—J. C. Woellner and Bischofswerder—Political Influence—The Jesuits and the Illuminati—Weishaupt—King Frederic William II....................59

*Appendix—*The Principles of the Yoga-Philosophy of the Rosicrucians and Alchemists...70

Chapter Seven—In the Pronaos of the Temple of the True Cross. The Cross and the Rose—Rosicrucian Rules—The duties of a Rosicrucian—The Secret Signs of the Rosicrucians—Rosicrucian Jewels—Rosicrucian Symbols—Signs from the Heart of the celestial Mother—Signs referring to the Divine child....................................71

Chapter Eight—Alchemy. The Science and Art of Alchemy—The Prima Materia—The Spiritus Universalis—The Secret Fire—The four alchemical rules—The five things necessary to observe in the practice of Alchemy—Axiomata Hermetica................................85

PREFACE.

QUITE a number of books dealing with the "History of the Rosicrucians" have appeared of late for the purpose of amusing and gratifying the curiosity of the mystery-loving reader; but it does not appear that they have proved to be very instructive, or that they have succeeded in throwing much light upon this perplexing subject; neither is it to be desired that the Rosicrucian mysteries should be publicly bawled out and exposed to the view of the vulgar; because they belong to that which is most holy and sacred in the constitution of man.

Books on true occultism are on the whole very useless things; because those who are in possession of occult knowledge will not require them; while those who have no such knowledge will not understand them; neither will they receive much benefit from such literature; because real spiritual knowledge must be found within one's own soul; it cannot be learned from books. The scientist, rationalist, and speculative philosopher deals only with, so to say, the candlesticks bearing the candles from which is emanating the light which they cannot see, neither can they see the candle; for the latter is representing the soul, whose light is the spirit.

Truly occult and Theosophical books ought to be prayers and poems; calculated to lift the heart and the mind of the reader up to the highest regions of thought, and aiding him to descend into the innermost sanctuary of his own being; so that he may become able to open the senses of his interior perception and grasp himself those divine ideals which are beyond the understanding of the semi-animal intellect; for spiritual truth cannot be brought down to that level; it requires, for its recognition, the rising up in the spirit to its own plane; neither can any man reveal to another the light, if the light does not reveal its presence to the investigator; all that a book can do is to aid the reader in opening his own eyes.

Little would it benefit us if we knew of the existence of sunlight only from reading about it in books, and were incapable to see the light and to enjoy the rays of the sun. What would it serve us if we theoretically knew all about the constitution of the terrestrial sun if we were encompassed by darkness? What good would it do to us to be informed about all the qualities of the divine powers of God, if we could recognise nothing divine within our own selves?

No man can show to another the light if the latter is incapable to see it himself; but the light is everywhere; there is nothing to hinder a person to see it, except his love for the darkness. His love for the illusions of his terrestrial phase of existence causes him to regard these illusions as real, and to relegate the Real to the realm of fancy and dream. Nevertheless, that which seems now the true light to him will be as darkness when his consciousness awakens to the perception of the light of the spirit.

As light is incomprehensible except by its contrast to darkness, I have not only selected some of the best portions of the writings of the ancient hermetic philosophers and mediæval "Rosicrucians"; but I have also taken the trouble to collect a few facts from the great storehouse of human follies to be found in the fools' paradise of the visionary and dreamer; but for those who earnestly wish to enter the path and to follow the Light, I have added some of the most precious gems, taken from the books of the sages; whose meaning will be incomprehensible to the would-be wise; while those who are unsophisticated will find therein a great deal of wisdom.

THE AUTHOR.

```
            F R O
            O U F
            R C U
            M I L
            A S G
MAGNUSVESTITH
ONORLAETUSLOQ
UORHOCNATIONI
            R E M
            A R I
            T A C
            A N T
            C D U
```

Chapter One

INTRODUCTION.

IN the popular books of to-day, dealing with the origin of religion, we find it stated that they originated from fear. It is described how our ancestors, while in a savage state, and being unacquainted with the revelations made by modern science, saw the lightning flash, and heard the noise of thunder and watched other natural phenomena, whose origin they could not explain, and how they came to the logical conclusion that such things must be produced by some extra cosmic supernatural and intellectual power, which might some day take a notion to destroy their possessions; and which must, therefore, be flattered and propitiated so that it might be kept in a good humour.

Such a scientific explanation of the origin of religion and the belief in God may satisfy the speculating brain of the rationalist and thinker, who, living entirely in the moonshine of his own imagination has no perception for the light of that knowledge which belongs to the spirit of man; but such a theory will not satisfy the heart in which there is still a spark of the divine life, and which, therefore, feels the presence of a universal and higher power that is not a product of nature, but superior to her. A religion having such a merely logical origin would be truly the religion of the devil, because it would be thoroughly false. It would be merely a system teaching how God may be cheated and eternal justice be made to come to naught. True religion has nothing to do with fear nor with logical speculation, and its true origin rests in the fundamental relation which the human soul bears to the divine origin of the spiritual power by which she is inhabited. It is the divine spirit in man itself, recognising and through the instrumentality of man the presence of the universal spirit in nature. This divine power is truly "occult," because it cannot be perceived by any external means, neither can its existence be logically proved to those who are not capable to feel it; it will for ever remain a mystery to the "Adam" of earth; because it is divine and can therefore be intellectually known to man only when he has entered into a state of divinity.

Nevertheless, it is a quality inherent in the nature of man that he wishes to know intellectually that whose presence he intuitively feels, and there have, therefore, at all times been men curious to know the nature of God, and attempted to break by their intellectual efforts a hole through the veil that covers the sanctuary of the great mystery, so that they may peep through it, and gratify their curiosity. From the vagaries of such speculators, visionaries and pseudo-philosophers has originated a false system of theology, mysticism, and superstition, which is even to-day often regarded as being Occultism and Theosophy.

The soul of man stands in the same relation to that spiritual power that fills the universe, as the flowers of the field to the light of the terrestrial sun. A plant deprived of life will sicken and die, and a soul in which the spirit of holiness does not exist will become degraded lower than the soul of the animals; because animals are not given to arguing; they act according to the laws of their nature, while the possession of an intellect enables man to act unnaturally, and in opposition to divine law.

But there have also been other men, who, by remaining natural and obedient to divine law, have grown into a state of spirituality superior to the merely intellectual state, and in the course of their interior unfoldment, their inner senses have become opened, so that they could not only intuitively feel, but also spiritually perceive this light of the spirit. Such men are the true Mystics, Rosicrucians, and Adepts, and with them the historian and antiquarian has nothing to do; because they are beyond his reach of investigation. A "History of Rosicrucians" could, at best, be a history of certain persons who "were supposed to have been spiritually enlightened." It would have to remain for ever uncertain whether a person mentioned in such a "history" had really been a Rosicrucian or not; because that which constitutes a man a saint and a sage does not belong to this earth and cannot be examined by mortal men; it is that part of man of which the Bible speaks when it is written, "We live upon the earth; but our soul is in heaven."

External investigation can only deal with external things; that whose existence depends on a form can deal only with forms; but all forms are merely fictitious to him who recognises by the power of his spiritual perception the truth which the form represents. The whole of nature is an expression of truth; but there are few who can realize the truth expressed in nature. We are all more or less caricatured images of the truth which we are originally intended to represent. As long as we have ourselves merely a fictitious existence, owing to the non-recognition of the truth within our own selves, we merely know the caricature which we represent, but not our true, real self.

Wisdom, as a principle, is inconceivable unless it becomes manifest in the wise, and only the wise are capable to recognise it. A man without knowledge knows nothing. It is not man in his aspect as a being without any principle who can know any principle whatever; it is always the principle itself that recognises itself in other forms. Thus, if a person wants to know the truth, the truth must be alive in him; if there is no truth in him, he can perceive no truth, neither within himself nor in external nature. For ever the truth is crucified between two "thieves" called "superstition" and "scepticism," and if we see only one of the crucified thieves, we are liable to mistake him for the truth; but the two forms of the thieves are distorted, or, to express it more correctly, the truth is distorted in them. Only when we are capable to recognise the straight form of the Saviour hanging between the two distorted thieves, will we see the difference and know where to search for the Redeemer.

For those in whom the truth has not yet become a living power, fictitious forms are necessary to show them the way, but the majority of the ignorant see only the fiction; there being no truth within themselves, there is nothing to perceive the truth in the form. For this reason the "Secret Symbols of the Rosicrucians" will for ever remain "secret" to all who have not the living truth within their own hearts, and they will not comprehend them, in spite of all the explanations produced. These, however, in whom the truth struggles to become alive and who are striving not merely for the gratification of their curiosity, but who love the truth for its own sake and without any personal consideration, may be aided a great deal by the study of the books of the Rosicrucians and their secret symbols, in the same way as a traveller in a foreign country may be aided by those who have travelled there before him and know the way. They can indicate to him the road through the desert and the places where sweet water may be found, but they cannot carry him, he is to do the walking himself.

Divine wisdom is not of man's making, neither is it invented by him. There is no other way to obtain it than by receiving it willingly within one's own heart. If it enters there, then will the storm of contending opinions subside, and the sea of thought be as clear as a mirror in which we may see the truth. Then will the truth itself become strong in ourselves, and we shall know God, not by reading a description of Him in books but in and through His own power, or, to express it in the words of the Bible, we shall attain knowledge of Him "by worshipping Him in Spirit and in Truth."

Like the allegorical language of the Bible and other religious books, the Rosicrucian writings are utter nonsense and incomprehensible, if taken in an external sense and applied from a material point of view. Merely external reasoning, far from being an aid in their understanding, is rather an obstacle in the way; but to him who looks at them with the understanding that comes from the spirit, they are full of divine wisdom.

The Rosicrucians say, "A person who knows Divine truth has attained the highest and desires nothing more; for there can be nothing higher than the attainment of the truth. In comparison with this treasure, wordly possessions sink into insignificance: for he who possesses the highest has no desire for that which is low; he who knows the reality does not care for illusions. Scientific and philosophical speculations in regard to what may possibly be true are useless to him who feels and perceives the truth; he does not need to speculate about that which he already sees and knows. He does not require great riches, for the wants of his physical form are few and simple, and moreover, by the action of the spirit within, radiating in an outward direction, the material principles composing his physical form become more and more sublimated and etherealized, and independent of the necessities of the material plane; until at last, having stripped off the last sheath of the gross and visible form, and having made that principle conscious which gives life within the visible inner body, he may live entirely in the latter, invisible to mortal eyes, independent of material conditions, an ethereal spirit surrounded by indescribable beauties, in possession of powers of whose existence mortal man does not dream— an ethereal spirit, but nevertheless a real and living man." (1.)

And, again, the Rosicrucians say of him who has tasted of the living water of truth, the true "Elixir of Life":—

"Blessed is he who is above want and poverty, above disease and death, who cannot be touched by that which gives pain, who does not require another roof over his head than the sky, no other bed than the earth, no other nutriment than the air, and who is above all those wants for which mortals are craving." (2.)

"God humiliates the vain and exalts the humble. He punishes the proud with contempt; but to the modest He sends His angels with

---

(1.) It will readily be perceived that all this refers to the "Inner Man," and not to his mortal physical frame. It is neither the physical body with its external senses, nor the perishing mind of man which can know divine truth. It is only divine truth in man that can know its own self. No man can attain true knowledge of any spiritual power, unless that power becomes alive in him and he identified with it. Occultism is not a question of what one should know, nor of what one should do; but of what one must *be*. If the inner man has become truly spiritual, not merely in his imagination, but in his will; then his awakened spirit will penetrate even through the physical form and change its nature in the same sense as darkness is consumed by light.

(2.) All this refers not to the man of terrestrial flesh; but to him who has been regenerated in the life of the spirit. The elementary body of man is not above disease and death; nor above that which gives pain. That body requires to be sheltered against the elements whereof it is made; and needs terrestrial food; but the man of the celestial kingdom is free. His home is as wide as his thoughts can reach, and his nutriment is the "Manna" from heaven.

consolation. He throws the evil disposed into a wilderness; but to the kind-hearted He opens the portals of heaven." (3.)

"Avoid the books of the Sophists; they are full of errors; for the foundation upon which their knowledge rests is their fancy. Enter the realm of the real, and divide with us the treasures which we possess. We invite you, not by our own choice, but by the power of the Divine Spirit whose servants we are." (4.)

"What does the animal know about intellectual pleasures? what does the Sophist know about the joys of the spirit? Would it not be a precious thing if we could live and think and feel as if we had been living and thinking and feeling ever since the beginning of the world, and were to continue thus unto its end? Would it not be delightful to know all the secrets of Nature and to read that book in which is recorded everything that has happened in the past, or which will exist in the future? Would you not rejoice to possess the power to attract the highest instead of being attracted by that which is low, and to have pure spirits instead of animals assembling around you?" (5.)

Are such powers attainable by man? It would be useless to attempt to prove it to those who have no desire to attain them; and even if it were proved, what would it benefit those who are poor to prove to them that there are others in possession of treasures which for the former do not exist? Can the existence of powers be proved to one who has no capacity for their perception or comprehension? Even a miracle would prove nothing except that something unusual and unexplained had occurred.

The *Fama Fraternitatis* says: "The impossibility to reveal such secrets to those who are not sufficiently spiritually developed to receive them is the cause that many misconceptions and prejudices have existed among the public in regard to the Rosicrucians. Grotesque and fabulous stories, whose origin can only be traced to the ignorance or malice of those who invented them, have been circulated and grown

---

(3.) "God" (according to Jacob Boehme) is the will of divine wisdom. He who rises up in his self-conceit will fall; because he will be full of his delusive knowledge, and the will of the Eternal cannot awaken divine wisdom in him. True humility does not consist in abject fear; but in the highest sense of dignity, such as can be felt only by him who feels that God is in and with him.

(4.) The "sophists" are those sceptical inquirers who diligently examine the external shell of the fruit that grows upon the tree of knowledge; without knowing that there is a kernel within the fruit. They persuade themselves that there is no kernel, and imagine that those who are capable to perceive by the power of the spirit the light that shines from the interior fountain, are dreamers; while they themselves little know that their own life is merely a sleep and their fancied knowledge a dream.

(5.) The spirit of man is not of this world; it belongs to eternity. There never was a time when the spirit of man was not; even since the beginning of creation; neither is its presence limited to this planet Earth. He who succeeds in merging his consciousness with that of the divine spirit that overshadows his personality, and which is his own real self, will know his past forms of existence and see the future; but the animal principles in man cannot partake of that state; they die and enter again into the *Chaos*, the storehouse for the production of forms.

in intensity and absurdity as they travelled through the ranks of the gossippers. Falsehoods cannot be eradicated without injuring the roots of the truth, and evil intentions grow useful to contradict the false statements made by the ignorant or wilful deceiver; but what is the testimony of the blind worth when they speak of what they believe they have seen and what value can be attached to the statements of the deaf when they describe what they believe they have heard? What does the untruthful know of the truth, the godless of God, the foolish of wisdom, and the unbeliever of faith? They may think that they are right, nevertheless they are wrong; they may accuse others of harbouring illusions, while they live in illusions themselves. Envy, hate, jealousy, bigotry and superstition are like coloured glasses, which cause him who looks through them to see nothing in its true aspect, but everything in coloured light."

Thus it appears that the "Rosicrucians," in speaking of their society, means something very different from any terrestrial and external organization of persons calling themselves, for some reason or other, "Rosicrucians"; but of a spiritual union, a harmony of divine and conspritual, but, nevertheless, individual powers, such as the angels are supposed to be, and which are not concerned in any history connected with the tomfooleries of external life.

It is of that spiritual "association" of which they speak when they say:—

"Our community has existed ever since the first day of creation, when God spoke the word, 'Let there be light,' and it will continue to exist till the end of time. It is the society of the children of light, whose bodies are formed of light, and who live in the light for ever. In our school we are instructed by Divine wisdom, the heavenly bride, whose will is free, and who comes to him whom she selects. The mysteries which we know embrace everything that can possibly be known in regard to God, Nature, and Man. Every sage that has ever existed has graduated in our school, in which he could have learned true wisdom. We have among our members such as do not inhabit this globe; our disciples are distributed all over the universe. They all study one book, and follow only one method of studying it. Our place of meeting is the temple of the Holy Spirit pervading all nature, easily to be found by the Elect, but for ever hidden from the eyes of the vulgar. Our secrets cannot be sold for money; but they are free to everyone who is capable to receive them. Our secrecy is not caused by an unwillingness to give; but by the incapacity to receive on the part of those that ask for instruction.

"There is only one eternal truth; there is only one fountain of love. Love cannot be given, it must be born in the human heart. Wherever the quickening takes place, we attend to the birth of divine love. We are in possession of a light that illumines the profoundest depths of the darkness and enables us to know the deepest of mysteries. We have a fire by which we are nourished and by which wonders may be performed in nature.

"Everything in this world is subject to our will, because our will is one and identical with the law; nevertheless, our will is free and bound by no law.

"Do you wish to become a member of our society? If so, enter within your own heart and hearken to the voice of the Silence. Seek for the Master within yourself, and listen to his instructions. Learn to know the Divinity that seeks to manifest itself within your soul. Throw away your imperfections and become perfect in God."

Chapter Two.

THE HERMETIC PHILOSOPHY.

Tria sunt mirabilia.   Deus et Homo.   Mather et Virgo.   Trinus et Unus.

THERE is only one eternal truth and consequently only one divine wisdom. If we wanted to trace the history of those in whom that wisdom became manifest back to their origin, we would have to step out of time and space and enter into eternity. We would have to go back to the first days of creation, when "the spirit of God moved upon the waters," when the "first initiator" (1) instructed a race of semi-spiritual beings, constituted very differently from the human beings as we now know them upon this planet. The externally reasoning historian speaks of the wisdom-religion of the ages, as if it were some system invented by man and evolved from the gradually unfolding speculative power of the reasoning intellect; but the Occultist knows that divine wisdom is eternal and always the same; all that differs is the form of its manifestation, according to the capacity of the minds in which it seeks for expression. A history of the doctrines of the Rosicrucians might, therefore, begin with an exposition of the doctrine of the Vedas or the ancient books of Egypt; but as these subjects have been extensively treated in H. P. Blavatsky's "Secret Doctrine" and other books, we will merely see in what shape the hermetic philosophy presented itself to the minds of the neoplatonic philosophers.

NEOPLATONISTS.

AMMONIUS SACCAS.

THIS philosopher, who lived about 190 A.D., was the founder of the *Neoplatonic School.* He was the son of Christian parents, and received a Chritsian education, but departed from this system and became a "philosopher." He gained a living by carrying burdens for pay, and yet he was one of the greatest philosophers of that age, and well acquainted with the Platonic and Aristotelian philosophy. His disciples were *Erennios, Origenes, Plotinus,* and *Longinus.*

PLOTINUS.

Plotinus was born at *Lykopolis* in Egypt in the year 205 A.D. He received his education at *Alexandria.* He took part in the war of the Emperor *Gordianus* in Persia, and went afterwards to *Rome,* where he established his school of philosophy. Here he obtained great renown and was respected by all. It is said that during the 26 years he lived in Rome he did not have a single enemy. Even the Emperor *Gallienus,* one of the greatest villians, respected and honoured him.

Plotinus fell sick. As the physician *Eustachius* entered the room in which Plotinus was dying, the latter exclaimed, joyfully, "I am now going to unite the God that lives within myself with the God of the Universe."

The mind of Plotinus was continually directed towards the Divine genius who accompanied him,—his own higher self. He cared little about his physical body, and having been asked about the day when the latter was born, he refused to tell it, saying that such a trifling matter was of too little importance to waste any words about.

Phenomenal existence was to him an error, a mistake, a low and undesirable condition, union with the Divine principle the highest aim of existence. He ate very little, took no meat, and lived a life of chastity. *Porphyry*, another one of the disciples of Saccas, having become envious of the renown of Plotinus, attempted to use black magic against him, but without success; and finally said that the soul of Plotinus was so strong that the most powerful Will directed against his soul could not penetrate it, and rebounded upon the sender. Plotinus, however, felt that magic influence, and expressed himself to that effect.

According to the philosophy of Plotinus, God is the foundation of all things. There is only one Substance; Matter and Form are merely illusions, or shadows of the Spirit. God is eternal and everywhere. He is pure light, a Unity, the basis of all existence and thought. The Mind (*voûs*) is the image of this Unity; it is, so to say, the image created by the Eternal by looking within itself. Thus the Mind is the product or creation of God, and yet God itself, and receiving its power from the latter. The Mind is the eternal activity of the Eternal. It is *Light*, primordial and unchangeable. Thought and every thinkable object exists within the mind. The world of Mind is the internal world; the external, sensual world is the external expression of the former. Mind being a Unity, and all beings and objects consisting of Mind substance, all are fundamentally identical, but they differ in form.

The activity by which the inner world of Mind came into existence is an interior power acting towards the centre. If an external world, corresponding to the inner world, is to come into existence, there must be another activity by which this internal activity is reversed, so as to be directed towards the periphery. This centrifugal activity is the *Soul*, a product or *reaction* of the centripetal activity of the Mind, in other words a product of *Thought*, entering within itself.

There is a universal law according to which something real may produce something approaching its own state of perfection, but not quite as perfect as itself, and therefore the activity of the soul resembles the activity of the mind, but is not as perfect as the latter.

The Soul, like the Mind, is living thought, but unlike the Mind, subject to continual change. The soul, unlike the mind, does not see things within her own self, but sees them in the mind. The activity of the soul is directed outwardly, that of the mind inwardly; the perceptions of the soul are not so clear as those of the mind. The soul, like the mind, is a kind of light; but while the light of the mind is self-luminous, that of the soul is a reflection of the former.

According to the eternal laws of order and harmony existing in the whole organism of Nature, all souls become after a certain time separated from the mind, or—to express it more correctly—the distance between the soul and the centre of mind increases, and they assume a more material state. Moving away from the Divine intelligence they enter the state of matter, they descend into matter. At each step towards materialization their forms become more dense and material, the souls in the air have an airy, those upon the earth an earthly material form. The activity of the soul produces other and secondary activities. Some of the latter have an upward tendency, others follow lower attractions. The upward-tending activities are Faith, Aspiration, Veneration, Sublimity, etc.; the downward tendencies produce reasoning, speculations, sophistry, etc.; the lowest activity of the soul is the purely vegetative power, sensation, assimilation, instinct, etc.

The ultimate aim of the activity of Nature is the attainment of self-knowledge. Whatever Nature produces in a visible form, has also a supersenual form, giving shape to gross matter, so that the form may become an object for recognition. Nature is nothing but a living soul, she is the product of a higher, interior activity, the Universal Mind. There is only one fundamental living power in Nature, the power to *imagine;* there is only one result of the activity of this power, *formation,* or perception of form, and the same process which takes place in Nature, takes place in the nature of man.

All formations of matter are produced by the soul residing therein. All forms are filled with an interior life, even if not manifested outwardly. The Earth is like the wood of a tree, wherein life exists; the stones resemble twigs which have been cut off from the tree. In the stars, as well as in the Earth, is Divine Life and Reason.

The sensual world and each existence therein has an interior soul, and this soul is all that is lasting about those forms; the external appearance is nothing more than an appearance.

The World of Intelligence, is an unchangeable living Unity wherein there is no separation by space or change in time. In that world exists everything that *is,* but there is neither production nor destruction, neither past nor future. It is not in space, and requires no space. If we say the world of intelligence is everywhere, we mean to express the idea that it is in its own being, and, therefore, within itself.

The world of Intelligence is the world of Spirit. There is a supreme Intelligence, wherein are germinally (potentially) contained all objects and all intellects, and there are as many individual intellects as can possibly be contained in that world of intelligence. The same may be said about the Soul. There is a supreme *Over-Soul,* and as many individual souls as can be contained therein; and the latter stand in the same relationship to the former as a species to the one class to which it belongs. There are different kinds of species in a class, yet all originate in the latter. Each species has a character of its own. Likewise, in the intellectual world there must be some certain qualities to produce souls of various kinds, and the souls must be in possession of various degrees of thought-power, else they would all be identical in every detail.

There is nothing absolutely without Reason in Nature, although the manifestations of the principle differ vastly in the various forms. Even animals, which seem to be unreasonable, possess a reason which guides their instincts. Everything that exists has its origin in Reason, and there can be nothing absolutely unreasonable in Nature; but there are innumerable modes in which Reason becomes manifest, because these manifestations are modified by external and internal conditions and circumstances. The inner, *spiritual* man is far more reasonable than the external one. In the external world Reason manifests itself as observation, logic and speculation; but in the world of intelligence Reason is manifest in *direct perception of the truth*.

The aim of the internal action of reason is to produce an objective form. As differentiation proceeds and the various powers unfold, they continually lose some of their attributes, and the ultimate products are less perfect than the original power; but the circumstances in which they are placed give rise to the origin of new attributes, and thus a step is made towards rising again into a higher state.

Thus the world of intelligence is a radiation from the fundamental original centre, and the world which we perceive with our senses is a product of the world of intelligence. The state of imperfection and mutability of all things in the external world is caused by their remoteness from the great centre. The Universe is a product of three fundamental principles of existence; it is a great *living* being or organism, in which all its constituent parts are intimately connected together, and no part in that universe can act without causing a certain reaction in all other, even distant parts because throughout the whole there is only *one* soul, whose activity, manifesting itself in all parts, constitutes the organism of the whole. All parts are connected together by that universal power which constitutes the *One Life* in the universe. All souls lead, so to say, amphibious existences. Sometimes they are attracted more to the sensual plane and become interwoven with the latter; at other times they follow the attraction of Reason, from whence they originated, and may become united with it. *The soul ultimately becomes divided*, the higher elements rise to the higher planes, the lower ones sink still lower when they are no more held up by their connection with the higher ones. Whenever the incarnation of a human being takes place, the soul furnishes the mortal body with some of her own substance, but she does not, as a whole, belong to the body; and only that part of the soul which has become thoroughly amalgamated with the body takes part in the pains and pleasures of the latter. Man's evil desires come only from that part of his soul, which is thus mixed with the body, and, therefore, the evil consequences of man's evil actions befall merely the animal man—that is to say, his living animal principle—but not the real man or the spirit, connected with the higher elements of the soul. The more the soul is attracted to the vulgar and low, the more grossly material will the organism with which she clothes herself become. After death the gross substances must be purified or destroyed, while the pure elements rise up to the source from whence they came, until the time for a new incarnation in a form of flesh has arrived. This process is repeated until the soul has attained sufficient knowledge to become inaccessible to the attraction of that which is low. In this sense man's terrestrial existence may well be looked upon as being a punishment for harbouring evil desires and inclinations. Intellectual labour is an activity belonging to a lower state of existence, and is necessary because the original faculty of the soul of directly perceiving the truth has been lost. If the soul desires to obtain this faculty again, she must free herself from all intellectual conceptions, and penetrate into the formless. If she desires to reach up to the original inconceivable fountain of all, she must leave her own conceptions behind, she must become free from all sensual perceptions and intellectual speculations, free of thought and speech, and live in a state of spiritual contemplation. That which is beyond intellectual conception can be seen, but can neither be conceived nor described in words. Seeing is better than believing, knowledge is better than logis; spiritual knowledge is *one*, but human science is a multiplicity, and has nothing to do with the eternal Unity, from which all things take their origin.

It is of the utmost importance that men should be instructed about their own nature, their origin, and their ultimate destiny; because an intellectual person is not inclined to undertake a labour, unless he is convinced about its usefulness. Spiritual perception is a power, which cannot be imparted, but which must be gained by effort.

If a person does not know that such a power exists, or if he cannot realize its usefulness, he will make no efforts to attain that state, his mind will remain without illumination, and he will not be able to see the truth. He may feel the existence of the truth, like a man may feel love for an unknown ideal, of which he does not know whether or not it exists; but he whose mind is illumined sees the object of his love, the light which illumines the world. This light is present everywhere. But it exists relatively only for those who are able to see, perceive, feel, and embrace it, by reason of their own similarity to it. To make the matter still more comprehensbile, let us say that if the soul throws off her impediments and enters that state again in which she originated from the Eternal, then will she be able to see and feel the Eternal. If, after having received these instructions, a person is too indolent to follow them, he will have no one to blame but himself if he remains in darkness. Let all, therefore, try to tear themselves loose from that which is low and sensual, and become united with the supreme power of God.

If you desire to find the Supreme, you must free your thoughts of all impressions coming from the external world, purify your mind of all figures, forms, and shapes.

God is present in all, even in those who do not recognise Him; but men flee from God, they step out of Him, or, to speak more correctly, out of themselves. They cannot grasp Him before whom they are thus fleeing, and, having lost themselves, they hunt after other gods. But if the soul progresses on the road to perfection, begins to realize her own higher state of existence, to know that the fountain of eternal life is within herself, and that she, therefore, has no need to hunt after external things, but can find all that is desirable in the divine element within herself; if she begins to understand that in that God within is her whole life and being, and that she must flee from the realm of illusions to live and exist in Him, then will the time come when she will be able to see Him, and to see herself as an ethereal being, illumined by a super-terrestrial light. She will see herself even as the pure Divine Light itself, as a God, radiant in beauty, but becoming dark again as her light is rendered heavy if it approaches the shadows of the material plane.

Why does not the soul remain in that state of light? Merely because she has not yet freed herself fully from the attractions of matter. If she has become entirely free of these attractions, she will remain in that light, and know that she is one with it. In this state there is no perceiver and no object of perception, there is merely perception, and the soul is that which she perceives. She is, for the time being, identified with the object of her perception, and, therefore, this state is something beyond the intellectual comprehension of man.

Having been united and identical with it, the soul carries its image within herself when she returns to herself. She then knows that during the time of her union with the Eternal she was the Eternal itself, and there was no difference between herself and the former. In herself there was no motion, no sensation, no desire after anything else, neither was there thought nor conception. She was exalted and resting in her own being, she was, so to say, rest itself, in a state surpassing all conceptions of beauty or virtue. A soul entering into this sublime state, in which there is no form and no image, cannot be supposed to enter anything illusive. A soul which sinks into illusions degrades herself, and enters the region of evil and darkness; but the exalted soul enters into herself; she is then neither in a state of being nor of non-being, but in one which is inconceivable and above all being.

MALCHUS PORPHYRIUS.

This philosopher was a disciple of *Plotinus*, and was born in *Batanea*, in Syria, in the year 233 A.D. He died at Rome in the year 304 A.D. He says that only one single time during his life did he succeed in obtaining his union with God, while his teacher Plotinus, was *four* times blessed in this manner.

Porphyry says, in regard to the Soul:—The embodied soul is like a traveller who has lived a long time among foreign nations, and has, therefore, not only forgotten the costumes of his own country, but also adopted those of the foreigners. When such a traveller returns from his voyage, and desires to be welcomed by his friends and relatives, he attempts to lay off his foreign manners, and to return again to his former way of acting and thinking. Likewise the soul, while banished from her celestial home, and being forced to inhabit a physical form, acquires certain habits from the latter, and if she desires to return to her former state, she must lay aside all she has adopted from her terrestrial form. She must try to put off not merely the gross physical mask in which she is dressed, but also her more interior envelopes, so that she may enter, so to say, in a state of nudity into the realm of bliss.

There are two poisonous sources from which man drinks oblivion of his former condition, and which cause him to become forgetful of his future destiny, namely sensual pain and sensual pleasure. By the action of these two, but especially by the action of the latter, desires and passions are created, and these attract the soul to matter and become the cause of her corporification. Thus the soul is, so to say *nailed to the body*, and the *ethereal vehicle* of the soul is rendered heavy and dense. We should avoid everything which may excite sensuality, because wherever sensuality is active, reason and pure intelligence cease their activity. We should, therefore, never eat for the mere pleasure of eating, but only eat as much as is necessary to nourish the body. Superfluous, and especially animal food, strengthens the bonds which bind the soul to matter, and withdraw her from the Divinity and from divine things. The wise, being a priest of God, should seek to remain free of all impurities while he is in the temple of Nature, and he should never so far forget his dignity as to approach the Source of all Life while he himself constitutes a grave for the dead bodies of animals. He should select for his nutriment only the pure gifts of his terrestrial mother. If we could avoid all kind of food, we should become still more spiritual.

In regard to the difference existing between *corporeal* and *incorporeal* things, Porphyry says:—"The Incorporeal governs the Corporeal, and is, therefore, present everywhere, although not as space, but in power. The corporeal existence of things cannot hinder the Incorporeal from being present to such things as it desires to enter into relation with. The Soul has therefore the power to extend her activity to any locality she may desire. She is a power which has no limits, and each part of her, being independent of special conditions, can be present everywhere, provided she is pure and unadulterated with matter. Things do not act upon each other merely by the contact of their corporeal forms, but also at a distance, provided they have a soul, because the higher elements of the soul are everywhere, and cannot be enclosed in a body, like an animal in a cage, or a liquid in a bottle. The universal soul, being essentially one and identical with the infinite supreme Spirit, may, by the infinite power of the latter, discover or produce everything, and an individual soul may do the same thing if she is purified and free from the body."

"The realm of the soul, being semi-material, has its inhabitants possessing semi-material (astral) forms. Some of them are good, others evil; some are kindly disposed towards man, others are malicious. Both classes have ethereal but changeable bodies; the good ones are masters of their bodies and desires, the evil ones are governed by the desires of their bodies. They are all powers for good or for evil, divine, animal, or diabolic invisible influences creating, by their interior activity, passions, desires, vices, and virtues in the souls of beings. The more evil they are, the more do their forms approach the corporeal state. They then live on the exhalations of matter; they induce men to murder and to kill animals, they enjoy the vapours arising from the victims, and grow fat by absorbing the ethereal substances of the dying. They are, therefore, always ready to incite men to wars and crimes, and they collect in great crowds in places where men or animals are killed."

Porphyry ridicules the idea that gods, being wiser, more powerful, and superior to man, could be coaxed, persuaded or forced to do the will of man or conform to his desires. He repudiates the theory that clairvoyance, prophecy, etc., were the results of the inspiration by external gods, but says that they are a function of the Divine Spirit within man; and that the exercise of this function becomes possible when the soul is put into that condition which is necessary to exercise it. "The consciousness of man may be centred within or beyond his physical form; and according to conditions a man may be, so to say, out of himself or within himself, or in a state in which he is neither wholly without nor within, but enjoys both states at once." He also states that there are many invisible beings, which may take all possible forms and appear as gods, as men, or as demons, that they are fond of lying and masquerading, and of pretending to be the souls of departed men.

It is said that Porphyry was several times during his prayers levitated into the air, even to the height of ten yards or more, and that on such occasions his body appeared to be surrounded by a golden light. "The gods are everywhere, and he whose soul is filled with such a divine influence to the exclusion of lower influences is, for the time being, the god which that influence represents, possessing his attributes and ideas. The nature of the union of the soul with God cannot be intellectually conceived or expressed in words; he who accomplishes it is identical with God, he is Divinity itself, and there is no difference between him and the latter. The gods are not called down to us by our prayers; but we rise up to them by our own holy aspirations and efforts; we are connected with them by the all-embracing power of love."

Jamblichus.

This philosopher was a disciple of Porphyry, and died about 333 A.D. He says:—

"If the soul rises up to the gods, she becomes god-like and able to know the *above* and the *below;* she then obtains the power to heal diseases, to make useful inventions, to institute wise laws. Man has no intuitive power of his own; his intuition is the result of the connection existing between his soul and the Divine Spirit; the stronger this union grows, the greater will be his intuition, spiritual knowledge. Not all the perceptions of the soul are of a divine character; there are also many images which are the products of the lower activity of the soul in her mixture with material elements. Divine Nature, being the eternal fountain of Life, produces no deceptive images; but if her activity is perverted, such deceptive images may appear. If the mind of man is illumined by the Divine Light, the ethereal vehicle of his soul becomes filled with light and shining."

Proclus.

Proclus lived at *Byzany,* 412—485. He was a hermetic philosopher and mystic, having often prophetical visions and dreams. It is said that he had the spiritual power of producing rain by his "prayer" and of preventing earthquakes. He was very pious and self-denying, and on some occasions his head seemed to be surrounded by a glory of light.

He says that the soul of man consists of many coats; some more dense, and others of a more ethereal character, each one being a fundamental principle, changeable only in regard to its form. "The soul can only return to her divine state after having been purified of her earthly desires. Her reason and free will must take part in the sufferings belonging to the material state, until she attains knowledge and becomes free from desires. For this purpose she clothes herself at certain periods in a physical form (reincarnates as a human being), until she has laid off her desires. The more the soul frees herself from her gross external coats (principles) the higher can she rise."

Hierocles.

This philosopher says:—"The intelligent soul-substance received from the *Demiurgos* (Logos) an inseparable immaterial body, and entered thus into being. She is, therefore, neither corporeal nor incorporeal, but comparable to the sun and the stars, which are the product of an immaterial substance. This soul-body, which human beings as well as "spirits" possess, is of a shining nature. The vehicle of the soul is contained within the material body of man; it breathes Life into the lifeless and soulless physical organism, and contains the harmony of the latter. The *Life Principle* of man is the inner being which produces the activity of Life in the organism. The inner man consists of an intelligent substance and an immaterial (transcendentally material) body. The visible material form is the production and image of the interior man. The external form consists of the animal, unintellectual, gross-material and ethereal bodies, a separation of living substance and dead matter is effected, and thus man may render himself capable of having intercourse with pure spirits.

During the year 529, the imperial bigot *Justinian* closed the schools of Philosophy at *Athens,* and their last representatives, *Isodorus, Damascius,* and *Simplicius* went to Persia. They expected to find in the East freedom of thought, tolerance, and wisdom. It was said that *Chosroes,* the King of Persia, was a philosopher, and they hoped to obtain his protection. But they soon found that the philosophy of that King was very superficial, and that he was a cruel, passionate, and ignorant tyrant, varnished over with some superficial learning. Disappointed, they returned to Greece.

This was the experience of the last of the Neoplatonic philosophers, such as were publicly known, and a long obscuration of the sun of wisdom took place, until a ray of light broke again through the clouds during the 15th century.

Chapter Three

MEDIAEVAL PHILOSOPHERS.

Centrum in Trigono Centri

THE external world is an image of the interior world. The astronomy of the visible starry sky is an external reproduction of astrological processes taking place in the invisible heavens, and the revolutions of the planets which are within the reach of observation by our physical senses, are symbols by means of which the action of spiritual powers existing in the universe are represented. As the earth has her seasons of heat and cold, according to her position which she occupies in regard to the sun, and as she approaches the sun at certain times and recedes at others, likewise there are regular periods at which the human mind seems to come nearer to the spiritual sun of divine wisdom, and there are other times when a period of darkness and materialism exists. During the times of perihelion, receptive minds will find it easier to rise up in their thoughts to the fountain of eternal truth; while during the aphelion it requires greater efforts to approach the divine luminary. During the time of the Middle Ages there appears such perihelion to have taken place, and a wave of spirituality was passing over the world, illuminating the minds of those who were receptive for wisdom; while in the minds of the vulgar it merely aroused the emotional element, causing among them an epidemic of superstition, which manifested itself on the external plane as the development of witchcraft and sorcery. There were many hermetic philosophers of great prominence living during those times. Foremost of all must be mentioned Theophrastus Paracelsus, of Hohenheim; Jacob Boehme, Cornelius Agrippa, Basilius Valentinus, Robert Fludd, and many others too numerous to be named. As the lives and the philosophy of the two former ones have already been explicitly dealt with in my other books, I will select from the rest the writings of Cornelius Agrippa as a type of what was taught by those mediæval philosophers.

MAGIC, ACCORDING TO CORNELIUS AGRIPPA.

Cornelius Agrippa of Nettesheim was born of a noble family at *Coeln (Cologne)* on September 14, in the year 1486. He was a philosopher, physician, lawyer, theologian, soldier, and also a statesman. He studied the Occult Sciences, and is said to have been a good Alchemist. He also organized at Paris a secret society for the purpose of studying the secret sciences. He drew upon himself the hatred and malice of the clergy, whose evil practices he desired to reform, and he was consequently denounced as a black magician and sorcerer, and there are even to-day nearly as many fabulous stories circulating about him as there are in regard to the reputed black magician, *Doctor Faustus*. He was an open enemy of the Holy Inquisition, continually persecuted by the latter, and therefore he had to change his place of residence very often. While only twenty-four years of age he wrote his celebrated work, "Occulta Philosophia," which in his riper age he greatly improved. His study of the occult side of nature led him to realize the fact that the truth cannot be found in illusions, even if they belong to the supersensual plane of existence, and he therefore says in his book, *"De Vanitate Scientiarum"*: "He who does not prophesy in the truth and power of God, but by means of dæmons and evil spirits, errs. He who produces illusions by magic spells, exorcisms, citations, conjurations, philtres, and other dæmoniacal methods deserves to be punished in hell."

Cornelius Agrippa made great effort to restore the true meaning of the term "Magic": a term which means the exercise of spiritual functions which are in possession of the *wise;* but the ignorant even to this day use the term "Magic," when they want to talk about Sorcery and Villainy, which is not wisdom, but the very thing opposed to it. In regard to his book he says: "I have written it in such a manner that those who are wise will find therein all the information they desire; but to the evil disposed and the sceptic the door to the mysterious realm will remain closed, no matter how hard they may struggle to enter it. If you possess the power of seeing with the eye of reason, the whole sublime magic science will appear before your sight, and you will know the powers which Hermes, Zoroaster, and Apollonius knew."

"The *Key* to the highest and divine philosophy of the mysterious powers of nature is reason. The brighter the sun of reason shines, the more powerful will the intellect grow, and the easier will it become for us to accomplish even the most wonderful things. But if the intellect is in the bonds of flesh, if it cannot overcome the errors received by inheritance and false education, it will be unable to penetrate into the divine mysteries of nature and God. He who wants to enter into the sanctuary must die. He must die to the world and to external sensual attractions, die to his animal instincts and desires. Not that by such a death the soul would become separated from the body; but the soul must be able to step out of the latter. Therefore *Paulus* writes to the Colossians: 'You have died and your life is hidden with Christ in God'; and at another place he says: 'I know a man (but whether he was in the body or out of the body I do not know, God knows it) he was exalted into the third heaven.' Such a death must he die who wishes to know God, and only few are privileged to do so."

"Whatever we read about the irresistible powers of the Magic Art, of the wonderful sights of the Astrologers, etc., will be found to be fables and lies as soon as we take those things in their external and literal meaning. Their external forms cover internal truths, and he who desires to see those truths must be in possession of the divine light of reason, which is in possession of very few. Therefore those who attempt to solve the problems of the divine secrets of nature by the reading of books will remain in the dark; they are led away from the light of reason by the illusive glare of their erring intellect; they are misguided by the tricks of external astral influences and by erroneous imaginations. They fall continually into error by seeking beyond their own selves that which exists within themselves. You must know that the great cause of all magic effects is not external to ourselves, but operating within ourselves, and this cause can produce all that the Magicians, Astrologers, Alchemists, or Necromancers ever produced. Within ourselves is the power which produces all wonderful things.

Nos habitat, non tartara, sed nec sidera coeli
Spiritus in nobis, qui viget, illa facit.

"Magic Science embraces a knowledge of the most sublime and exalted truths, the deepest mysteries in nature, the knowledge of the nature of matter and energy, of the attributes and qualities of all things. By uniting the powers of nature and combining the lower with its corresponding higher counterpart the most surprising effects may be produced. This science is therefore the highest and most perfect of all; she is a sacred and exalted philosophy the culminating point of all."

Agrippa regards nature as being a trinity; an elementary (corporeal) astral and spiritual world, and the lower principles are intimately connected with the higher ones, forming thus four more intermediary states; that is to say, *seven* in all.

The cause of all activity in the universe is the omnipresent principle of *Life* (being identical with the Will), a function of the universal spirit. This life principle causes the ethereal Soul to act upon the gross element of Matter.

"The Spirit—the *Primum mobile*—is self-existent and is motion; the body, or the element of matter, is in its essence without motion, and differs so much from the former that an intermediary substance is required by which the Spirit can be united with the body. This intermediary spiritual substance is the soul, or the *fifth essence* (quinta essentia) because it is not included in the four states of matter, which are called the four elements, but constitutes a fifth element, or a higher state of matter which is perceptible to the physical senses. This soul of the world is of the same form as the world; because as the spirit in man acts upon all the members of his body by means of man's soul, likewise the universal spirit by means of the soul of the universe pervades and penetrates all parts of the latter. There is nothing in the world which does not contain a spark of this universal power; but spirit is most active in those things or beings in whom the activity of soul is strongest.

This astral spirit can be rendered very useful to us if we know how to separate it from the other elements, or if we use such things as contain an abundance of it. There are certain things in which this principle is not so deeply sunk into or so strongly amalgamated with the body as it is in others, and such things act powerfully and may produce their counterparts.

This is the great alchemical agent, and in it are contained all productive and generative powers. If this spirit is extracted from gold or silver and united with some other metal it transforms the latter into gold, respectively silver.

There is such a great harmony and unity in nature that every superior power sends its rays through intermediary links down to the lowest, and the most inferior thing may rise up through the scale to the highest. Thus the lowest is connected with the highest comparable to a string of a musical instrument, which vibrates in its whole length if touched at one end. If the lower is acted on it reacts upon the higher, and the highest corresponds to the lowest.

A thing of very small size may produce a great effect (as may be seen by the growth of a tree from a seed), but this cannot take place with an elementary quality (physical force). The hidden powers may accomplish a great deal, because they are the properties of the form to which they belong; but the elementary (mechanical or physical) forces, being material, require a great deal of matter to produce great effects upon matter. The powers belonging to the form are called *occult* powers, because their causes are hidden; that is to say, even the sharpest intellect cannot thoroughly conceive of their nature, and what the philosophers know about them they have learned rather by observation and experience, than by intellectual reasoning.

God created man in His own image. The universe is the image of God and man is the image of nature. Man is therefore, so to say, the image of the image; in other words a *Miscrocosmos,* or little world. The world is a reasonable, living, and immortal being; man is equally reasonable, but he is mortal, or at least divisible. *Hermes Trismegistus* says that the world is immortal, because no part of it is ever annihilated. Nothing is ever annihilated, and if "to die" means to be annihilated, then is "dying" a term without any reason for its existence; because there is no death in nature. If we say that a man dies, we do not mean to imply that anything of that man perishes; we only mean to say that his body and soul become separated from each other. The true image of God is His Word, Wisdom, Life, Light, and Truth; they exist through Him, and the (spiritual) soul is their image. This is the reason why it is said that *we* (man in its primitive purity as a spiritual being) have been created in the image of God, and not in the image of the world or its creatures. God can neither be touched with the hand, nor be heard with the external ear, nor be seen with the external eye, and likewise the spirit of man can neither be seen, heard, or touched in this manner. God is infinite and cannot be overpowered by anything, and likewise is man's spirit (spiritual soul) free and can neither be forced nor limited. In God is contained the whole world and everything existing therein, and likewise in the will of man is contained every part of his body. Man being thus stamped and sealed in the image of God as His counterpart, necessarily clothed himself in a form, representing the true image of nature. He is therefore called the second or little world; he contains everything contained in the great world, and there is nothing existing in the latter which is not also truly existing within the organism of man. In him are contained all the elements (principles), each principle according to its own qualities; in him is the ethereal *astral* body, the vehicle of his soul, corresponding to the firmament of the world; in him is the vegetative power of plants, the principle of sensation, manifest in the animal kingdom, the divine spirit, divine reason, and the divine mind. All this is contained in man, united to a unity and belonging to him by divine right. Man is therefore called by the Bible "the whole creation," and in his aspect as the Microcosm he contains not only all parts of the world, but also contains and comprehends the divinity itself.

The natural Soul is the *Medium* by which the Spirit becomes united with the flesh and the body, through which the latter lives and acts and exercises its functions. This Medium is intelligent, but also so to say corporeal; or to express it perhaps more correctly, the soul takes part in the materiality of the physical body. This is the doctrine of all hermetic philosophers. Man consists of the higher, the intermediary, and the lower principles. The higher ones are called the illuminated spiritual soul, and Moses speaks of it figuratively as having been breathed by God into the nostrils of man. The lowest is the animal soul (anima sensitiva). The apostle Paulus calls it the animal man. The intermediate part is the rational soul which connects the animal soul with the divine mind and takes part in the nature of the two extremes. This part, to become free, must be separated from the lower elements by the power of the *Will* of which the apostle says, that it is living and cutting like a sword. The divine principle never sins and never consents to sin; but the animal principle sinks continually lower in animal desires unless it is held up by the divine spirit. The highest part of ourselves is never subject to punishment, knows nothing of the sufferings of the lower principle; but returns after being separated from the lower principles to its divine source; but that part which is called the rational soul, and which being free, may choose between the higher or lower, will, if it continually clings to the highest, become united with God and immortal in him; but if the intellectual principle clings to that which is evil, it will become ultimately evil, and grow to be a malicious demon.

God is the centre of the world and enters the heart of man, like a sun-ray. As the spirit of God descends, it surrounds itself with an ethereal substance, forming the *Astral body,* the vehicle of the soul (the fiery chariot of the soul). From the centre of the heat the spirit radiates into all parts of the body and pervades all its members, combining its own vehicle with the natural heart of the body and with the soul substance generated within the heart. By means of the soul it mixes with and amalgamates with the fluids (the blood, nerve currents, etc.), and with all organs of the body. The soul is therefore equally near to all organs, although she radiates from one organ into another in the same sense as the heat of a fire is intimately connected with air and water, if it is carried from fire to water by means of the air. In this way we may form a conception of the process, by which the immortal spirit by means of its immortal ethereal vehicle may be enabled to adhere to and mix with a dense, mortal, material body. If by disease or otherwise the connection between different parts of the same organism is interrupted, the spirit returns again to the heart. If the life-principle leaves the heart, the spirit departs with the ethereal vehicle and the physical organism dies.

The first Light in God is beyond intellectual conception, and can therefore not be called a conceivable light; but as it enters the mind it becomes intellectual light and may be intellectually conceived. Entering into the soul it may not only be conceived, but also understood. It is incorporeal. When it enters into the ethereal vehicle it takes form, invisible to the physical senses; but when it penetrates the elementary (physical) organism, it becomes also visible to the external perception. By this gradual progression of this divine Light from Spirit into dense Matter our spirit may obtain great power. It is possible that if the thoughts of the wise are directed with great intensity upon God, the divine light illuminates the mind and radiates its rays through all the parts of the dark and gross body, causing even the latter to become illuminated like a luminous star, and to change its attraction to the earth, so that it may be raised up into the air, and thus it has happened that even the physical bodies of men have been carried away to some distant locality. So great is the interior power of the spirit over the external body that the former may lift the latter up and take him to that place where man's thought travels or where he desires or dreams to be.

Man's power to think increases in proportion as this ethereal and celestial power or light penetrates his mind, and strengthening his mental faculties, it may enable him to see and perceive that which he interiorly thinks, just as if it were objectively and eternal. Spirit being unity and independent of our ideas of space, and all men having therefore essentially the same spirit, the souls of men existing at places widely distant from each other may thus enter into communication and converse with each other exactly in the same manner as if they had met in their physical bodies. In this state man may perform a great many things in an exceedingly short period of time, so that it may seem to us as if he had required no time at all to perform it. But not everybody can do so; it can only be done by those whose imagination and power of thought is very strong. Such a man (an

Adept) is able to comprehend and understand everything by the light of the universal power or guiding intelligence with which he is spiritually united.

But if imagination possess such a power that it cannot be impeded or restrained by the obstacles presented by time or distance, if it can even communicate itself to the heavy physical body and carry the latter with it; then it will be reasonable to believe that thought becomes still more powerful if it becomes free and may follow its natural inclinations, instead of being held back by the attractions of the sensual plane. In each man there is such a power, which is the inherent property of his soul by right of the divine origin of the latter; but this power is not equally developed in all men, but stronger in some, weaker in others, and according to the state of its development the possibility to use it differs in different individuals.

By this power two persons being bodily far distant from each other may exchange their thoughts, or one may impress his thoughts upon another, and such a power may be used for good or for evil purposes. Weak-minded persons may thus be fascinated by stronger minds, or be made to fall in love with the person by whom they are thus fascinated. The instrument of fascination is the spirit, and the organ by which it eminently expresses itself is the eye. Thus the spirit of one person may enter the heart of another by way of the eyes, and kindle a fire therein which may burn and communicate itself to the whole body. If two persons look into the eyes of each other, their spirits come in contact, and mix and amalgamate with each other. Thus love may be caused by a look in a moment of time, like a wound caused suddenly by an arrow. The spirit and the blood of a person thus affected then turn towards him who fascinated it, like the avenging spirit and the blood of a murdered person turns against the murderer.

The passions of the soul which adhere to the imagination may, if they are sufficiently strong, not only produce changes in the organism to which they belong, but also be transferred upon another organism, and thus impressions may be made by the will of a person upon the elements and external things, and thus diseases of the soul or body may be caused or cured. The state of the soul is the principal cause of the condition of the external body. A strong, exalted soul, stimulated by a strong and active imagination, may not merely cause health or disease in her own organism, but also in that of others with which she comes in contact. Evil disposed persons may exert a very evil influence upon others by their look. The invisible forces emmanating from the soul through the eye are much more powerful, stronger, hotter, and more active than the emanations of the physical body. The soul-force of a person entering within the soul sphere of another acts therein not less strong than it would act if it had originated in the latter. By such means one man may exert an influence upon the mind and character of another.

The spirit may accomplish a great deal by the power of *Faith*. This power is a firm confidence or conviction, based upon the knowledge that one can and will accomplish his purpose. It is a strong, unwavering attention which gives strength to the work, causing, so to say, an image in our mind of the power which is necessary to accomplish the work, and of the work which is to be accomplished in, by, and through ourselves. We must, therefore, in all magic operations, apply a strong will, a vivid imagination, a confident hope, and a firm faith; all of which combined will assist in producing the desired result.

It is well known that if a rich person has confidence and faith in his physician, he is more liable to be benefited by the latter than if he mistrusts him, and often the presence of the physician in whom the patient has faith benefits the latter more than the remedies which he uses. The presence of a spiritually-minded physician who possesses a strong soul, and who desires to help the patient, is a power which is often sufficiently strong to change the pathological activity of the soul-elements of the patient (of which the physical processes taking place in the organism are merely the external expression), and thus to restore the patient. Every physician ought therefore be a magician in a certain sense. He ought not to doubt in the least that he will be successful in that which he attempts to accomplish. He ought not even to permit a thought of the possibility of a failure to enter his mind; because as a firm faith may accomplish wonderful things, likewise doubt disperses the active power of the operator and renders it ineffective. In such a case the spiritual activity vibrates, so to say, between two extremes: it lacks the projecting impulse to enter the physical organism of the patient, it becomes diffused in space and is lost.

In this power of the spirit over the element of matter by means of the soul rests the power of certain signs, images, formulas, incantations, words, etc., and many wonderful experiments may thus be produced. The activity of the spirit strengthens the soul; by the will and imagination of the spirit the soul receives strength to act upon matter.

There is a spiritual power residing in the soul of man which enables the latter to attract, influence, and change things. If the power of the soul mounts to a certain height she may overpower the elements which hold her in bonds; for that which is *above* attracts and subjects that which is *below*, and the latter partakes of the changes of the former. Therefore, a man who has rendered himself capable to receive celestial gifts, by making use of the aspirations (functions) of his soul and employing natural things, may influence another being who is less spiritually strong, and force him to obey.

He may cure another by the power of his will or cause him to be sick or kill him; he may make him joyful or sad, fill him with fear, admiration, respect, veneration, etc.

The root from which all such effects spring is a strong and decided will supported by the spiritual influence coming from and through the heart. An opposing spiritual activity will, if the latter surpasses the former in strength, neutralize or repulse it, or weaken its influence.

If a man becomes subject to a fascination, it is not his intellectual principle, but his sensual (animal) soul which is thus affected. The intelligent and spiritual part in man cannot be thus magically influenced. If the organism of a man is suffering it suffers according to its animal and terrestrial, and not in his spiritual or celestial aspect. The intelligent and spiritual part of man can merely know that such influences are acting upon the lower principles by a certain sensation which is communicated from the lower to the higher elements. Intelligent man feels the influence which is exercised by external conditions upon his animal constitution; but he is not himself subject to their influences. Everything belonging to the *above* moves that which is next to it *below* according to its degree and order, not merely in the visible, but also in the invisible part of nature. Thus the Universal Soul moves the individual souls, the Mind acts upon the animal, and the animal upon the vegetative principle. Each part of the world acts upon every other part, and each one is capable to be moved by another; and upon each part of the lower world acts the higher world, according to the attributes and conditions of the former, just as one part of the animal organism acts upon another.

There is an art, known only to few, by which the purified and faithful (intellectual) soul of man may be instructed and illuminated, so as to be raised at once from the darkness of ignorance to the light of wisdom and knowledge. There is also an art, by which the knowledge gained by the impure and unfaithful may be taken away from their mind and memory and they thus be reduced to their former state of ignorance.

Apuleius says that the human soul may be put into a state of sleep, so that she will forget her terrestrial conditions and turning her whole being towards her divine origin, she will become illuminated by the divine light, and not only be able to see the future and to prophesy it correctly, but also to receive certain spiritual powers. On such occasions the divine inspiration and illumination may be so great, as even to communicate itself to other persons near, and to influence them in a similar manner.

Persons in a state of receptivity or passivity may become *mediums* through which divine demons (influences) may be attracted within the body of man and cause men to perform wonderful things. If the soul of such a person breaks away from the bonds of the body and surrenders herself to the power of imagination, she may become the habitation of demons of a lower order, which may enable her to perform extraordinary things. Thus we may see that a person who has never had any instructions in painting may suddenly exercise that art and produce an artistic work, etc., etc. If the soul enters entirely the intellectual sphere, she may become the habitation of another class of demons and obtain great knowledge in regard to human and external things, and man may thus become suddenly a great philosopher, physician, orator, etc., without having learned those things; but if the soul rises up entirely to the region of divinity, she may become the habitation of divine spiritual influences, and obtain a knowledge of divine mysteries.

Only those who are pure-minded and spiritual can possess true magic powers. Thought is the supreme power in man, and pure spiritual thought is the miracle-worker within him. If the thought of man is bound to the flesh, deeply amalgamated with it and occupied with animal desires, it loses its power over the divine elements, and therefore among those who seek to exercise magic powers there are few who succeed. If we desire to become spiritually developed we must try to find out how we can free ourselves of our animal instincts and desires and become rid of our sensuality and passions, and we must, furthermore, attempt to rise up to a state of true spirituality. Without accomplishing these two propositions we will never rise up to that state which is necessary to obtain magic powers, which result from the spiritual elevation and dignity of man.

We should therefore attempt to remove all external impediments which are in the way of our spiritual development and live in a state of purity. Our thoughts should be continually directed inwardly and within ourselves; for within ourselves is the element of consciousness, knowledge, and power. Nothing hinders us to develop and exercise our own powers, except our misconceptions, imaginations, and external desires. Therefore the divine influences will only come to him who liberates his soul of all such hindrances, carnal desires, prejudices, and hallucinations. A diseased eye cannot bear to look at the light; an impure soul is repulsed by the divine light of truth.

Such a process of development and unfolding is not accomplished at once, but requires time and patience; a neophyte cannot immediately understand the mysteries of initiation when he enters the sacred precincts. The soul must be gradually accustomed to the light until the power of spiritual thought is unfolded, and the latter being, continually directed towards the divine light, becomes at last united with it. If the soul is perfectly purified and sanctified she becomes free in her movements; she sees and recognizes the divine light and she instructs herself, while she seems to be instructed by another. In that state she requires no other admonition or instruction except her own thought, which is the head and guide of the soul. She is then no more subject to terrestrial conditions of time, but lives in the eternal, and for her to desire a thing is to possess it already.

C. Agrippa here adds the following instructions, copied from Boëthius:—

"The guides on the road to perfection are Faith, Hope, and Charity, and the means to attain this object are Purity, Temperance, Self-

control, Chastity, Tranquility of Mind, Contemplation, Adoration (Ecstasy), Aspiration, and Virtue."

If the highest state of spiritual development is attained, the spirit, endowed with the highest spiritual activity of the soul, attracts the truth, and perceives and knows at once the conditions, causes, and effects of all external and internal, natural and divine things. It sees them within the eternal truth like in a mirror of Eternity. By this process *Man*, while he still remains in eternal nature, may know all that exists in the internal and external world, and see all things, not merely those which are, but also those which have been, or which will exist in the future, and, moreover, by being united and identified with the divine power (*The Logos*), he obtains the power to change things by the power of his (spiritual) *Word*. Thus man being within nature may be above her and control her laws."

Those who are able to read the works of *Cornelius Agrippa* by the light of internal reason, will see that a single page of his books contains more wisdom than whole libraries filled with the speculations and theories of our modern philosophers, and his name and doctrines will be remembered and admired when all the illusions and hallucinations of the latter will have sunk into the oblivion which they deserve.

Chapter Four.

AMONG THE "ADEPTS."

A BELIEF in the existence of persons endowed with abnormal or extraordinary psychic faculties or magical powers, by which they can produce wonderful effects, such as are not to be explained by the commonly accepted theories of external science, is nothing new. The Bible and the "Acta Sanctorum" are full of accounts of so-called "miracles," a term which signifies something wonderful, but for all that not anything contrary to the laws of nature. Such "wonders" are performed by the power of the spiritually awakened will. The Yoga philosophy gives a specification of these powers, and describes how they may be acquired.

To those powers belongs the art of making oneself invisible; of leaving one's body at will and returning to it again; of projecting one's soul to a distant place; of prolonging physical life for a long period of time; of transforming base metals into pure gold by alchemical means; of creating subjective illusions which appear to the spectators as objective realities, and of performing numerous other feats, such as belong to the department of Magic, white or black.

There is sufficient evidence going to show that during the time of the Middle Ages there were numerous people existing in whom such psychic faculties had been more or less developed. It was a time during which the imagination of the people as a whole was more active and more directed toward the supersensual and metaphysical aspect of the world. There was more of the true faith, and likewise more superstition to be found than at present, and faith as well as fear are active powers, capable to produce results on the astral plane. From the true faith, the result of spiritual knowledge, spring the powers of the Adept; from fear and superstition, the phenomena of obsession and sorcery. Persons in possession of magic powers, and especially those who were supposed to know the secrets of Alchemy, were called "Adepts," "Rosicrucians," or "Philosophers," and the greatest of them were supposed to belong to some secret and mysterious society, called *"the Brotherhood of the Golden and Rosy Cross."*

If we allow a great deal of poetical liberty in the descriptions of the members of this fabulous order, charging it to the fruitful imagination of the writers living at the time of the "knights errant," nevertheless, there remains a considerable amount of historical evidence going to show that there were persons endowed with abnormal powers; although there is no evidence whatever that they were united among themselves by any external association or sect. Neither would such a farce ever be necessary among those whose internal senses were opened, and who would be drawn together by the ties of the spirit. Having the power of interior perception, they would surely not need any external passwords and signs. The true brothers of the Golden and Rosy Cross were and still are a spiritual society, and therefore the effort made at that time of finding a real and living, indisputably true Rosicrucian, were as unavailing as was at a more recent period the effort made by a certain London society of proving the existence of real and living Adepts.

The Rosicrucians have been celebrated in prose and in verse; and their virtues have been extolled by some, while others have denounced them as impostors. Some writers describe them as beings of a superior character, possessed of apparently supernatural knowledge and powers, as men of noble appearance and exercising an invisible but irresistible influence over all with whom they come into contact. They describe them as having the power to read the hearts of men, and to cure the diseases of their bodies by wonderful medicines, or merely by the touch of their hands. They are loved by all and they love all; but their hearts are invulnerable to sexual love. They never marry. They are sometimes described as being of fabulous age, and still appearing in the full vigour of manhood; as being great travellers and speaking the language of each country where they temporarily reside, as fluently and correctly as if it were their own native tongue; as possessing the power of rendering themselves invisible, and again, as often appearing unexpectedly, when their presence is most urgently needed. They are possessed of immense treasures, and have the power to transmute base metals into gold, and yet they despise riches and are contented to live in poverty. They are the wisest of all men, and the knowledge of even the most learned cannot be compared with what they know. They do nothing whatever for the purpose of obtaining fame, for they are dear to ambition; nevertheless their fame spreads wherever they appear. They are universally honoured, but they seek not for honour, and prefer to remain unnoticed. Palaces are at their disposal, but they prefer the hut of a beggar. They are not proud of their personal attributes, but it is the majesty of the divine principle manifesting itself in them, and shining even through the material envelope called the physical body, which surrounds them with an aura commanding the respect and veneration of all who approach. The glory of supermundane light which shines through their forms is so great that they may even appear luminous in darkness.*

---

* Before us is a paper, printed in Leipzig, dated May 26th, 1761, which gives the latest news from *Köln* (Cologne). It says: "The two prophets who have been imprisoned in this place are still keeping the attention of our citizens on the alert. The court has not yet decided what shall be done. It is useless to chain them, because they possess the wonderful power of bursting even the strongest chains, as if they were threads of linen, and they have done so in the presence of many. They can even in the darkest night see all objects.

The following is taken from a book entitled *"Hermippus Redivivus,"* which we will abbreviate as much as possible.

The *Sieur Paul Lucas*, who, by the order of Louis XIV., travelled through Greece and Africa in search of antiquities, says, "Being at Broussa, we went to a little mosque. We were introduced into a cloister, where we found four Dervishes, who invited us to their dinner. One of these, who said that he was of the country of the Usbeks (a Tartar tribe) appeared to me more learned than the rest; and *I verily believe he spoke all the languages of the world.* After we had conversed for a time in the Turkish language, he asked me whether I could speak Latin, Spanish or Italian. We then spoke in talian; but he noticed by my accent that this was not my mother tongue, and when I told him that I was a native of France, he spoke to me in as good French as if he had been brought up at Paris. I asked him how long he had stayed in France, and he answered that he had never been there, but that he desired to visit that country. This man was so learned that, judging from his discourse, he seemed to have lived at least a century; but according to his external appearance he was not more than thirty years of age.

"He told us that he was one of seven friends who had wandered all over the world with a view of perfecting their studies; that at parting they always appointed another meeting at the end of twenty years in a certain town, and that the first who came would wait for the rest. I perceived that Broussa was the place appointed for their present meeting. There were a few of them present already, and they seemed to converse with each other with a freedom which spoke of old acquaintance rather than merely accidental meeting. We spoke of religion, natural philosophy, chemistry, alchemy and the Kabala. I told him that the latter, and especially the notion of the 'Philosopher's Stone,' were considered by modern savants as mere chimeras. He seemed to know all about it, and answered: 'The true sage hears all things without being scandalized at them; but though he may have so much politeness as not to shock any ignorant person by his denial when they talk of such things; yet, let me ask you whether you think that he is obliged to sink his understanding to a level with vulgar minds because they are not able to raise their thoughts to an

---

in their prison, because there is *an unearthly light shining around their heads* and coming out of their eyes, which illuminates their surroundings. They seem to be young men, and yet they say that they were at Constantinople in the year 1453, at the time of Mohamed II.; they say that they were intimately acquainted with the last Christian emperor at that place, Constantine Palaeologus, and they are in possession of letters written by him and his wife and sister. They say that at the time when they were at Constantinople they were already over 300 years of age. They speak Persian and Chinese and other languages fluently; they live on nothing but a little bread and water. They performed some wonderful cures in the neighbouring villages before they were arrested; savage dogs and wild animals appear to treat them with reverence; they seem to be well acquainted with the books written by the ancient philosophers, and talk about Pythagoras with great respect. We do not know what to think about these men. Etc., etc."

altitude equal to his? When I speak of a sage, I mean that kind of a man to whom alone the title "philosopher" properly belongs. He has no sort of tie to the world; he sees all things die and revive without concern; he has more riches in his power than the greatest of kings, but he tramples them under his feet, and this generous contempt sets him even in the midst of indigence above the power of events.'

"I said: 'With all these fine maxims, the sage dies as well as other people. What imports it, therefore, to me when I die, to have been either a fool or a philosopher, if wisdom has no prerogative over folly, and one is no more a shield against death than the other?'

"'Alas!' he answered, 'I see you are absolutely unacquainted with our sublime science, and have never known true philosophy. Learn from me, then, my friend, that such an one as I have described dies indeed, for death is a debt which Nature enacts, and from which therefore no man can be exempt; yet he dies not before his utmost time is fixed. But then you must observe that this period approaches near a thousand years, and to the end of that time a sage may live. He arrives at that end through the knowledge he has of the true medicine. Thus he is able to ward off whatever may impede the animal functions of his body or injure the temperature of his nature; and is enabled to acquire the knowledge of whatever comes within the cognizance of man.

"Aboriginal man knew the secrets of Nature by the use of his reason, but it was this same reason which blotted his knowledge again from his mind, for having attained this kind of natural knowledge, he began to mingle with it his own notions and ideas. This created a confusion which was the effect of a foolish curiosity, and he reduced thereby the work of the Creator to a state of imperfection; and this is the error which the true sage attempts to redress. The other animals act only by their instinct, which they have preserved as they obtained it at first, and they live as long now as they did when they first came into existence. Man is a great deal more perfect than they; but has he still preserved that prerogative which he had in the beginning, or has he not lost long ago the glorious privilege of living a thousand years, which, with so much care, he should have studied to preserve? This the true sages have accomplished, and that you may no more be led into mistakes, let me, assure you that this is what they call the *Philosopher's Stone* which is not a chimerical science, but a real thing. It is, however, known to a few only, and indeed it is impossible that it should be made known to the most of mankind, whom avarice or debauchery destroys, or whom an impetuous desire of life prematurely kills.'

"'Surprised at all I heard, I said: 'Would you, then, persuade me that all who have possessed the Philosopher's Stone have likewise lived a thousand years?' 'Without doubt,' answered he, gravely, 'for whenever a mortal is favoured with that blessing, it depends entirely on his own will whether he shall reach that age of a thousand years, as in his state of innocence the first man might have done.'

"I took the liberty to mention the illustrious Flamel, who, I said, had possessed the Philosopher's Stone, but was now dead as far as I knew. As I mentioned that name, he smiled at my simplicity, and said with an air of mirth: 'Do you really believe Flamel is dead? No, no, my friend, do not deceive yourself, for Flamel is living still. It is not above three years ago since I left him and his wife in the *Indies*, and he is one of my best friends.' He was going to tell me how he made Flamel's acquaintance, but stopping himself, he said: 'That is little to the purpose. I will rather give you his true history with respect to which, in your country, I daresay, you are not very well acquainted.'

"A little before the time of Flamel there was a Jew of our fraternity; but as through his whole life he had a most ardent affection for his family, he could not help desiring to see them after it once came to his knowledge that they were settled in France. We foresaw the danger of his voyage, and did all we could to persuade him not to undertake that journey. We succeeded for a while in detaining him; but at last the passion of seeing his family grew so strong upon him that he went. At the time of his departure, he made us a solemn promise to return to us as soon as it was possible. He arrived at Paris, and found there his father's descendants in the highest esteem among the Jews. There was also a Rabbi, who was a true philosopher at heart, and who had long been in search of the great secret. Our friend did not hesitate to make himself known to his relatives, he entered into friendly relations with them, and gave them an abundance of light.

"'But as the matter requires a long time to prepare it, he put into writing the whole process, and, to convince his nephew that he had not told him falsehoods, he made the "projection" in his presence of some ninety pounds of base metal, and turned it into pure gold. The Rabbi, full of admiration, did all he could to persuade our brother to remain with him, but in vain; for the latter had made up his mind not to break the promise to return to us. When the Jew found this out, he changed his affection into hatred, and his avarice stifling the admonitions of his conscience, he resolved to extinguish one of the lights of the universe. Dissembling his black design, he begged the sage to remain with him only for a few days. He then executed his execrable purpose of murdering our brother, and made himself master of his medicine.

"'Such horrible actions never remain very long unpunished. Some other crimes he had committed came to light, the Jew was imprisoned, convicted, and burned alive.

"'Soon after this a persecution of the Jews began in France. Flamel, who was more reasonable than his enraged countrymen, and whose honesty was known, became a friend of the Jews, and a Jewish merchant entrusted him with all his books and papers, among which were those of the criminal who had been burned alive, and also the book of our brother; which had never been carefully examined by the merchant. When Flamel examined that book, his curiosity became aroused by certain figures contained therein, and he began to suspect that it contained great secrets. He got the first leaf, which was written in Hebrew translated, and from the little he learned from that, he became convinced that his suspicion was well founded; but knowing also that great caution was necessary, he took the following steps: He went into Spain, and, as Jews were settled in many parts of that country, he applied in every place to which he came to the most learned, and engaged each of them to translate a leaf of the book. Having thus obtained a translation of the whole, he returned to France. When he came home, he undertook with his wife the prescribed labours, and in the progress of time they arrived at the secret, by which they acquired immense riches, which they employed in building public edifices, and in doing good to a great many people.

"'Fame is often accompanied by great dangers; but a true sage knows how to extricate himself from all kind of perils. Flamel saw that he was in danger of being suspected to possess the Philosopher's Stone, a suspicion which might have caused the loss of his liberty, if not that of his life, and he thought of means to escape all danger. By his advice, his wife pretended to be dangerously sick, and when it was reported that she had died, she had already safely passed the frontier of Switzerland. They buried in her place a wooden image in one of the churches which he had founded. Some time afterwards he used the same stratagem for himself and joined his wife. You know that there could have been no great difficulty in doing this, since in every country, if a man has sufficient money, physicians and priests are always at his service, ready to say or do whatever he directs them. He moreover left a last will and testament, directing that a pyramid should be erected to his memory and that of his wife. Since that time both have led a philosophic life, residing sometimes in one country and sometimes in another. This, depend upon my word, is the true history of Flamel and his wife.'"

The well-known fact that the Adepts and alchemists of the middle ages were continually subject to persecutions, to imprisonment, punishment, torture and death, is the cause that the names of only few of them became publicly known. One reputed alchemist was the *Count de Saint Germain*, who lived in 1770 at the Court of France. He appeared to be about forty years of age; some said he was ninety, he himself gave his age as being 370 years. He possessed the art of making artificial diamonds and precious stones, he was clairvoyant, could read people's thoughts and foretell future events. He possessed an "album," in which many of the most celebrated persons of the sixteenth and seventeenth centuries had signed their names; he was able to write with both hands at one and the same time, with each on different subjects.

A somewhat similar character was the *Count Cagliostro*, whose physical form was born in Italy and received the name *Giuseppe Balsamo*. The latter was incarcerated in the castle *San Angelo at Rome*, and is believed to have died in one of its dungeons. The problem of Cagliastro will not be solved by our historians until they study the true nature of man in its normal and abnormal aspects, when they may, perhaps, discover the fact that two personalities may inhabit one physical organism, and that a man may, perhaps, be a *Cagliostro* at one time and a *Balsamo* at another.*

I have carefully read the proceedings of the trial of the renowned *Count Cagliostro* before the tribunal of the inquisition in Rome, and I have found no proof whatever of his having been an impostor. To everyone acquainted with even the elementary teachings of occultism, the phenomena which occurred in his presence do not appear at all unexplainable, or as having been the products of imposture; but what appears wonderful is the illogical consequence and ignorance of the witnesses for the prosecution, who admit the occurrence of phenomena in his presence, which could not have been produced by his tricks, while in the same breath they denounce him to be an impostor.

To arts of this kind belongs that of making pure gold or silver artificially, of transforming base metals into nobler ones; of preparing a *Universal Panacea* out of the principle of Life; of curing all diseases; of preparing a lamp which, by the manner in which it burns, indicates the state of health of an absent friend, with whom it is sympathetically connected; of producing a similar sympathetic or magnetic connection between a person and a jewel, a tree, or a mirror; of producing a living miniature image of the world in a closed glass globe; of causing the forms of vegetables or animals to reappear out of their ashes after they have been burnt; of producing artificially man (Homunculi) without the assistance of a female organism; of preparing a fluid, which rises and falls within the bottle where it is contained, according to the increasing or decreasing moon; of preparing a glass wherein it will thunder, and lightning will appear, whenever the same takes place in the air; of producing an inextinguishable

---

* Whether or not the body of a person may be inhabited simultaneously or alternatively by two different individualities, may be a matter for doubt; but the phenomena of obsession and hypnotism go to show that this is not impossible. Cagliostro said that he was born in the East, and it is certain that he had connections there; nevertheless, it was proved that he was born in Italy, and that his name was Balsamo. This would, of course, convict him at once among the ignorant of his times and among our writers of encyclopædias as being an impostor. Nevertheless, a more definite knowledge of the true constitution of man might explain the mystery. That which is the fundamental reality in man, is the will. The phenomena of so-called hypnotism show that the will of one person may be made to act in another, and during the time that a person is obsessed by the will of another, he is also under the influence of the memory of the latter. Those acquainted with occult laws will not find it incredible that the person of Balsamo was influenced and used by some eastern human spirit, whose name was Cagliostro, and that during such times Balsamo believed himself to be, and actually was, Cagliostro. Modern spiritualism has a legion of similar facts.

magic fire, an ever-burning lamp; a magic mirror, where events can be seen taking place in any other part of the world; a *perpetuum mobile*, whose rotation is caused by the rotation of the earth; a divining rod, for finding water or minerals, or whatever one wishes to find; a magic ring, which warns the wearer of any approaching danger, and reveals to him many secrets; of causing love or hate at will; of making pearls, diamonds, or any other jewels, which cannot be distinguished from natural ones, or causing them to grow larger; of obtaining power over the elemental spirits of Nature and causing them to render services; of causing the astral spectres of dead persons to appear and talk and answer questions, and many other similar feats, too numerous to mention.

We call that wonderful which is not within our experience, and the causes of which we cannot explain; we are daily surrounded by marvels, and witnessing the most marvellous phenomena, the causes of which we cannot explain; but we do not look at them with a sceptical eye, nor are we at all surprised that they occur. On the contrary, we should be extremely surprised if they once ceased to occur; this merely because we are accustomed to see such things every day. We are surrounded by phenomena of an occult and magic nature, and we live in a laboratory of alchemy. We see how out of a hard little stone—kernel or seed—a germ appears, and grows into a big tree, although we are sure that there was no such tree in the kernel; and what would be still more astonishing if it were not of daily occurrence, is that out of a certain kind of seed a certain species of plant only will grow, and no other. We see how out of an egg a living bird appears, and yet if we examine the same kind of egg as long as it is fresh, and open it, we find therein nothing living, and nothing that resembles a bird. We also know that the parent bird does not put a bird into the egg after it is laid, for we may hatch out eggs by artificial heat, and thus produce birds out of the egg, and there is surely no bird in the heat. We see how out of a vegetable substance animal substance can grow, for we feed our cattle on grass, hay, and corn, and yet we are certain that there is no flesh in the grass or corn. We see the ever-burning light of the sun spending its heat year after year. We know of nobody who supplies him with fuel, and yet it seems to have always the same temperature. We know that the globe whereon we live revolves and flies with tremendous velocity through space, and yet we do not feel it move, nor do we fall head foremost down in the abyss of space when at night it turns the dark side away from the sun; we see that the storm blows down houses and trees, and yet that which does the damage is nothing but thin air; we see the body of water of our rivers and lakes, and if we attempt to step on its surface we sink; but a few weeks or months afterwards we may try it again and find it as hard as rock, able to bear the weight of the skating crowd. There are a thousand other similar marvels in Nature, too numerous to mention.

There are many stories told of the Adepts, and the wonderful things they sometimes performed; how, in mid-winter, they caused beautiful flowers to grow out of the floor of a room, or produced a shower of roses in places where no roses were to be found; how some of them were seen simultaneously in two different places speaking and acting in each; how they sometimes were attended and served by "supernatural" beings appearing in human forms; how they were sometimes able to read the future, or see what was going on at a place hundreds of miles away from them; how they could speak languages which they had never studied; knew the contents of books which they had never read; could swallow poison without being harmed; make themselves invisible and visible at will, etc., etc. But the most interesting parts of our research, and at the same time the most pertinent to our object in view, will be historical accounts referring to their ability to make pure gold in an artificial manner—or, to speak more correctly, to transmute other metals into gold, and make gold grow. We shall therefore give a few abbreviated accounts of such authenticated facts:—

1. The following account is taken from the *acta* of the judicial faculty of Leipzig, whose legal decision was given in August, 1715. (Responsio Juridica Facultis Juridicæ Lipsiensis.) A few years ago a man arrived late in the evening at the residence of the *Countess of Erbach*, the castle of *Tankerstein*, and asked to be permitted to enter it, and to hide there a few days, as he had accidentally killed a deer belonging to the *Palatine* of *Palatia*, who was, therefore, pursuing him to take his life, and he asked to be protected. The Countess at first refused; but when she saw the man she was so much impressed with his noble appearance that she consented, and the stranger was given a room, where he stayed for a few days. After that he asked for an interview with the Countess, and when admitted to her presence, he expressed his thanks for the protection given to him, and offered that, as a token of his gratitude, he would transmute her silver ware into gold. The Countess at first could not believe that such a thing was possible, but she at last consented to have an experiment made with a silver tankard, which the stranger melted and transmuted into gold. She thereupon sent this gold to the city and had it tested by a goldsmith, who found it to be gold of the purest kind. She then permitted the stranger to melt and transmute all her silver spoons, plates, dishes, etc., into gold, which he did, and finally he took his leave and went away, having received a comparatively small sum of money as a gift from the Countess. Soon after this event, the husband of the Countess, who seems to have been a spendthrift, and who had been away from home for several years, serving as an officer in some foreign country, returned, because he had heard that his wife had become suddenly rich. He claimed half of the gold for himself, but the Countess refused to acknowledge his claims. The case came, therefore, before the Court, and the husband supported his claims by the fact that he was the lord of the territory (Dominus territorii)

upon which the castle belonging to his wife was located, and that according to the laws of the country all treasures found upon that land were lawfully his. He therefore requested that the gold should be sold, and from the proceeds new silver ware should be bought for the Countess, and the surplus be given to him. The defendant claimed that artificially produced gold could not come under the consideration of a law referring to buried treasures, and that therefore the said law could not be applied in her case; that, moreover, the silver had been transmuted into gold for her own benefit, and not for that of another, and she begged the Court to be permitted to remain in undisturbed possession of it. The Court decided in her favour.

2. Another authenticated case is that of an Adept by the name of *Sehfeld*, who lived in *Rodaun*, a small place in the vicinity of *Vienna*. He made gold out of tin and spent it freely. The proprietor of the house where he resided, a man named *Friedrich*, gained the confidence of the Adept, and told his family about the doings of Sehfeld. The consequence was that soon rumours and gossip began to spread. Sehfeld was accused of sorcery, and appealed for protection to the Austrian Emperor, saying that he was engaged in making certain chemical colours of which he possessed the secret. It is said that Sehfeld paid 30,000 florins into the Imperial Treasury to obtain this protection, which he enjoyed for several months. Friedrich and the members of his family often were present when Sehfeld made gold, and they say that after melting the tin, he sprinkled a small quantity of a red powder upon the molten mass, when the latter began to foam and exhibited all kinds of colours. After an hour or so it was allowed to cool, and all the tin was then transmuted into pure gold. One day Friedrich attempted to make the experiment himself. Having obtained some of the red powder from Sehfeld, he melted the tin while Sehfeld was absent, and sprinkled the powder upon it; but the latter had no effect upon the tin and did not mix with it. After a while, Sehfeld entered the room where the experiment was made, and as he entered the mass began to foam and turned into gold. The security which he enjoyed did not last long, for after a few months new rumours were put into circulation, the envy, greed and jealousy of the neighbours were aroused, he was accused of practising unlawful sciences, and he was arrested at night and imprisoned in the fortress of *Temeswar*, where he remained over a year, sternly refusing to tell his secret, and saying that no amount of physical torture would be able to make him reveal it. The governor of the fortress of *Temeswar, General Baron von Engelshofen*, was so much charmed by the noble appearance and open character of Sehfeld, that he went to Vienna and spoke to the Emperor about Sehfeld, declaring his opinion that the latter was innocent. The Emperor soon afterwards, while hunting boars in a forest near Rodan, sent for Friedrich, and received from him a detailed account of his experiences with Sehfeld, and became convinced

that the latter was not a villian; but he would not believe that he was able to make gold, and expressed his doubts to that effect. Upon this, Friedrich, who was an honest man, exclaimed, "Oh! your Majesty, if at this moment God were to come down from heaven, and say, 'Friedrich, you are mistaken; Sehfeld cannot make gold!' I would answer him, 'Dear God, it is nevertheless true that he can make it, because I know it to be so.'" Upon this, the Emperor, struck with the sincerity of the man, ordered that Sehfeld should be permitted to go where he pleased, and make whatever experiments he choose; but that he should not leave Austria, and should always be accompanied by two trustworthy officers who should never permit him to go out of their sight. Two of the best and most trustworthy officers belonging to noble families were selected for that purpose. He made several little excursions in their company; but not long afterwards Sehfeld and his two guards disappeared and never returned, nor has any trace of them ever been discovered. The historian adds that it is not probable that those two rich and noble officers would have sacrificed their career and also their reputation by thus deserting without having a sufficient cause or inducement to do so. Researches made in the house of Friedrich seemed to indicate that Sehfeld prepared his *red powder* out of some sky-blue minerals, probably some sulphuret of copper.

3. An apothecary at *Halle* made the acquaintance of a stranger, whom he found to be in possession of some chemical secrets. Having been invited to visit the stranger in his lodgings he went there, and after having talked about Alchemy, the claims of which the apothecary denied, the stranger showed him a certain *red powder*, and offered to give some of it to the apothecary so that the latter could make an experiment himself. With a very little spoon he took some of the powder out of the box wherein it was contained, but the apothecary objected that such a small quantity would not be sufficient to make the experiment. Upon this the stranger threw the powder back into the box, wiped the spoon, to which some of the powder adhered, on a piece of cotton, wrapped the cotton in a paper, and gave it to the apothecary, telling him that even this would be sufficient for that purpose. Having returned home, the apothecary took a big silver spoon, melted it in a crucible, and threw the cotton upon it. The molten metal began immediately to boil and to foam, and to exhibit the most beautiful colours. After a while he took the crucible from the fire and poured the metal into a mould. The next morning he examined it and found that it was the purest gold, and there were some ruby-red drops on the top, which seemed to have been the surplus of the red powder which the metal had not absorbed. The apothecary hurried immediately to the lodging of the Adept to tell him of his success; but the latter had gone, and no one knew where he went. A sum of money, more than sufficient to pay for his lodging, was found upon the table in his room. The silver which the apothecary

employed in this experiment weighed 1¼ ounces, and the gold which he gained weighed 1½ ounces, which he sold to a goldsmith for 36 *thalers*. The gain in weight was, therefore, 20 per cent., which may be accounted for by the fact that the specific gravity of gold is greater than that of silver. Unfortunately, the *ruby-red pearls* on the surface of the gold were lost during the excitement caused by the discovery that the mass was actual gold, else they might have been used to transmute a far greater quantity of silver into gold.

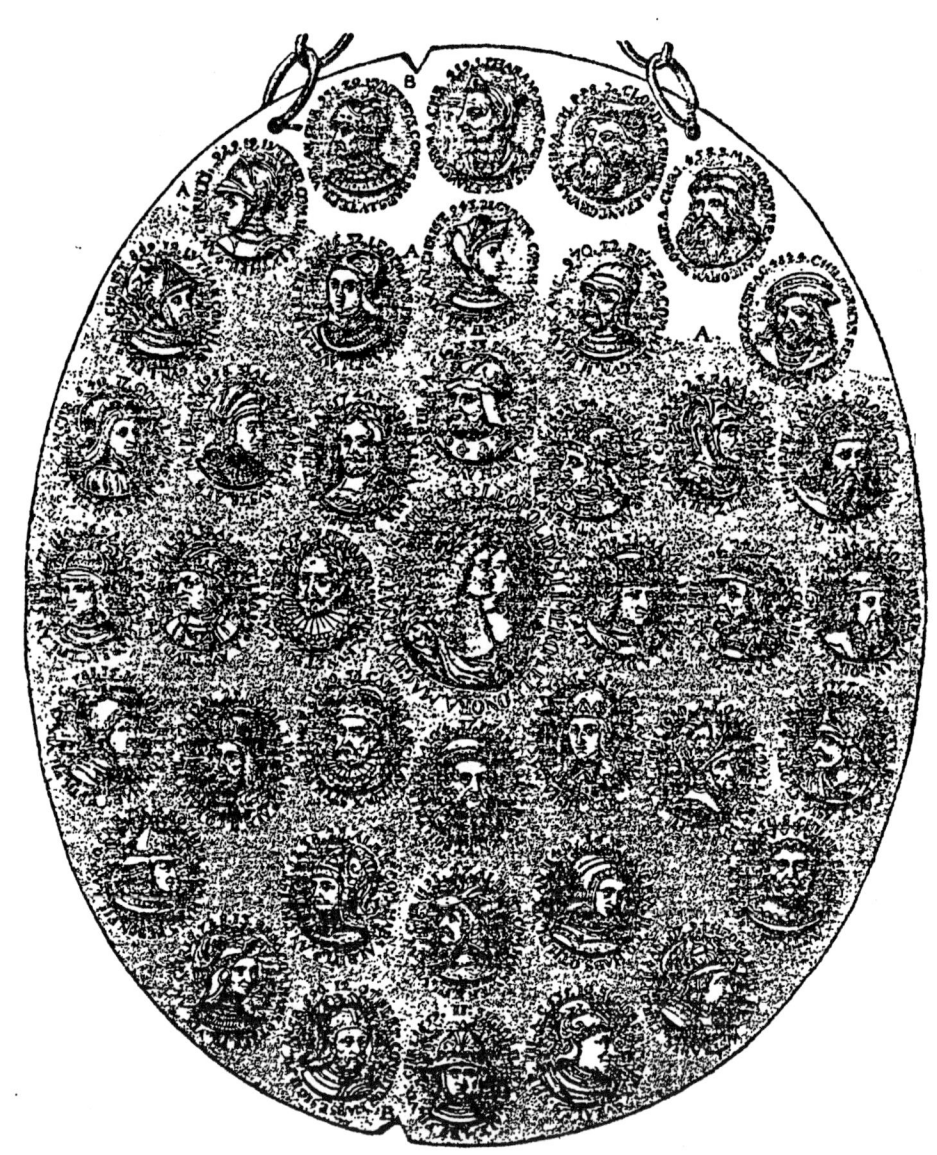

4. During the reign of the *Emperor Leopold*, a monk of the Order of St. Augustine, named *Wenzel Seiler*, found a certain *red powder* in his convent, which proved to be the "*Red Lion*" of the Alchemists. By means of this powder, Seiler transformed a quantity of tin into

gold in the presence of the Emperor and his Court. The Emperor ordered that certain medals were to be made of this artificially produced gold, and he divided them out among the noblemen of his Court. He also, as a reward, gave to that monk the title of *Freiherr von Rheinburg,* and appointed him as master of the Imperial mint in Bohemia. The medal, of which one is now in the family of *Count Leopold Hoffmann,* in *Brieg,* shows upon the top the bust of the Emperor Leopold, with the following words:—"*Leopoldus Dei Gratia Romanorum Imperator semper Augustus Germaniæ Hungariæ et Bohemiæ Rex.*" The reverse side is not stamped, but there is engraved thereon a verse, saying:—

Aus Wenzel Seilers Pulvers Mach
Bin ich von Zinn zu Gold gemacht.

5. The most indisputable proof (if appearances can prove anything) of the possibility of transmuting base metals into gold, may be seen by everyone who visits Vienna; it being a medal preserved in the Imperial treasury chamber, and it is stated that this medal, consisting originally of silver, has been partly transformed into gold, by alchemical means, by the same Wenzel Seiler who was afterwards made a knight by the Emperor Leopold I. and given the title Wenzeslaus Ritter von Reinburg.

The medal is of oval shape; its long diameter is 37, and the short one 40 centimetre. Its specific gravity is 19·3, and its weight 7,200·4 grammes. Its value is estimated to correspond to 2,055 Austrian ducats.

As indicated in the accompanying figure, about one-third of the upper part is silver, and the remaining part gold. The two incisions were made in 1883, for the purpose of examining the medal, to see whether it was pure or merely gilded. The examination was made on request of Professor A. Bauer, of Vienna.

One side of the medal shows the portraits of the ancestors of the Emperor, up to King Pharamund, the other side has the following inscription:—

Sacratissimo
Potentissimo et invictissimo
Romanorum imperatori
Leopoldo I.
Arcanorum naturæ scrutatori curiosmo
Genuinum hoc veræ ac perfectæ
Metamorphoseos metallicë
specimen
pro exiguo anniversarii diei nominalis
mnemosyno
cum omnigenæ prosperitatis voto
humillima veneratione offert et dicat

Joannes Wenzeslaos de Reinburg
numini majestatique eius
devotissimus
anno Christi MDCLXXVII. die festo
S. Leopoldi
ognomine pii olim marchionis Austriæ
nunc autem patroni augustissimæ
Domus austriacæ
Benignissimi.

It seems, however, that there is nothing perfectly reliable in this world of illusions, and it is therefore necessary to state that Wenzel Seiler was afterwards regarded as an impostor, and sent back to his monastery. Later on, however, the Emperor received him again into his favour, and even paid his numerous debts, the existence of which is quite incomprehensible if he actually had the power to make gold by alchemical means.

Chapter Five

THE ROSICRUCIAN "ORDERS."

WHY is there so much perplexity about the mysterious order of the Rosicrucians? Let us ask in return, Why is there so much perplexity about that mysterious being called "Man"? The answer is that man is a spiritual being, inhabiting the spiritual world, which he has never entirely left; while the terrestrial personality in which he manifests himself during his earthly life is an inhabitant of this planet. That which the historian and the scientist know about man is merely that which refers to his physical body; while nothing is known to them about his real self. To imagine that such knowledge is true anthropology is like imagining that we know all about a man if we once see the coat which he wears. Likewise the true Rosicrucians, whether they still walk upon the earth in a visible form, or whether they inhabit the astral plane, are spiritual powers, such as are beyond the reach of examination of the externally reasoning historian or scientist. They are people who, as the Bible expresses it, "live upon the earth, but whose consciousness is in heaven."

The vulgar sees only the external form, but not the spirit which is the true inhabitant of that form. To discern the latter, the power of spiritual discernment is required. The coat which a man wears does not make the man; to pour water over a person does not make him a true Christian, and to have one's name entered into the register of some society calling itself "Rosicrucian," does not endow one with the rosy and golden light of love and wisdom that comes from the unfoldment of the "Rose" within the centre of one's soul.

But it is far easier to undergo some external ceremony than to die the mystic death which is required for the purpose of passing through the "Gates of Gold"; it is easier to profess a creed than to acquire true knowledge; and for this reason we find during the Middle Ages not less than at this present time many people who imagine that they could be made into Rosicrucians and Adepts, by joining some society dealing with mystical subjects.

In the beginning of the 17th century Germany was overrun, not only by monks and nuns and religious fanatics of all kinds, but also by a great many impostors and adventurers. There were pretended Alchemists, Astrologers, Fortune-tellers, and there was a universal mania among the people to pry into the secrets of Nature, and to enrich themselves by alchemical processes, or, if need be, by the help of the devil. This epidemic of superstition and folly seemed to require a strong remedy, and as foolish people are not accessible to reasonable arguments, it occurred to some sharp-witted mind to try the more caustic remedy of sarcasm. There appeared in the year 1614 two pamphlets, written by the same author, entitled, *"Universal and General Reformation of the Whole Wide World,"* and the *"Fama Fraternitatis; or, Brotherhood of the Laudable Order of the R.C.* (Rosicrucians), *a message to the Governments, nobles, and scientists of Europe."* This book was out of print during the last century, and Frederic Nicolai, in Berlin, had it reprinted in the year 1781, falsifying, however, its date, inserting 1681 instead of the correct date, and "Regensburg" instead of "Berlin." Another edition of the *Fama Fraternitatis* appeared at Frankfurt-on-Maine in the year 1827, and to this was added an additional part, entitled *"Confessio."*

These books, soon after they first appeared, made a great impression upon the public mind, and were immediately translated into several languages. The *Universal Reformation* is a satirical work. Its most interesting contents are an account of the meeting of a supposed Congress for the purpose of reforming the world. The story is as follows:—At the time of the Emperor Justinian, *Apollo* takes a look at the world, and finds it to be full of vices and wickedness. He therefore makes up his mind to call together a meeting of all the wise and virtuous men of the country to consult together how this evil might be remedied. Unfortunately, among all of them there is none to be found who is possessed of sufficient virtue and intelligence to give the desired advice. Appolo therefore assembles the seven ancient sages of Greece and three Romans, *Marcus, Cato,* and *Seneca.* A young Italian philosopher, by the name of *Jacob Mazzonius,* is appointed secretary. The congregation meets in the delphic Palatium; and now follow the speeches which were held. The sages talk the most egregious nonsense. *Thales,* for instance, advises that a window should be inserted in the breast of every man, so that the people could look into his heart. *Solon* has become a communist, and wants to divide out all the public and private property, so that all should have equal parts. *Bias* proposes to prohibit all intercourse between the people, to destroy the bridges and to forbid using ships. *Cato* desires that God should be asked to send another deluge, to destroy the whole feminine sex and all males over 20 years of age; and to request Him to invent a new and better method of procreation. All the sages dispute and contradict each other, and finally it is resolved to cite the diseased century and make it come into court, so that the patient may be closely investigated. The century is brought in. It is an old man with a healthy-looking face, but having a weak voice. They examine him, and find that his face is painted, and a further investigation shows that not a single part of his body is without some disease. The savants then come to the conclusion that they cannot cure him; but they do not want to adjourn without having it appear that they had done something very useful and important, so they impose a new tax upon cabbage, carrots and parsley. They publish the document with a great deal of swagger and self-praise, and the delighted people jubilate and applaud.

The meaning of this pamphlet, which was written for the purpose of throwing ridicule upon a certain class of people who wanted to improve the world at once and to show the absurdity and impossibility of such an undertaking, was plain enough, and it seems incredible that its purpose should have been misunderstood. That there were any people who took the matter seriously shows the extreme ignorance and want of judgment of the common people of those times, and forms an interesting episode for the student of history and intellectual evolution. The other pamphlet which accompanied the former is the celebrated *Fama Fraternitatis*. The *Universal Reformation* threw ridicule upon the self-constituted "world-reformers," and this second pamphlet now invites these would-be reformers to meet, and it, at the same time, gives them some useful hints as to what they might do to attain their object; advising them that the only true method for improving the world is to begin by improving themselves. This pamphlet being like the other one, a satire upon the would-be reformers and so-called Rosicrucians, might, for all that, have been written by a genuine Rosicrucian, for it contains true Rosicrucian principles, such as are advocated by the Adepts. It shows the insufficiency of the scientific and theological views of those times. It ridicules the imbecility of the pretended Alchemists, who imagined that by some *chemical* process they could transform lead into gold; but in doing so it gives good advice, and under the mask of divulging the laws and objects of some mysterious Rosicrucian Society, it indicates certain rules and principles, which afterward formed the basis of an organised society of investigators in Occultism, who adopted the name *Rosicrucians*.

Added to this, *Fama Fraternitatis* is the story of the "pious, spiritual, and highly-illuminated Father," Fr. R. C. *Christian Rosencreutz*. It is said that he was a German nobleman, who had been educated in a convent, and that long before the time of the Reformation he had made a pilgrimage to the Holy Land in company with another brother of this convent, and that while at Damascus they had been initiated by some learned Arabs into the mysteries of the secret science. After remaining three years at Damascus, they went to Fez, in Africa, and there they obtained still more knowledge of magic, and of the relations existing between the macrocosm and microcosm. After having also travelled in Spain, he returned to Germany, where he founded a kind of a convent called *Sanctus Spiritus*, and remained there writing his secret science and continuing his studies. He then accepted as his assistants, at first three, and afterwards four more monks from the same convent in which he had been educated, and thus founded the first society of the Rosicrucians. They then laid down the results of their science in books, which are said to be still in existence, and in the hands of some Rosicrucians. It is then said that 120 years after his death, the entrance to his tomb was discovered. A staircase led into a subterranean vault, at the door of which was written, *Post annos CXX. patebo.* There was a light burning in the vault, which however, became extinct as soon as it was approached. The vault had seven sides and seven angles, each side being five feet wide and eight feet high. The upper part represented the firmament, the floor the earth, and they were laid out in triangles, while each side was divided into ten squares. In the middle was an altar, bearing a brass plate, upon which were engraved the letters, *A. C. R. C.*, and the words, *Hoc Universi Compendium vivus mihi Sepulchrum feci.* In the midst were four figures surrounded by the words, *Nequaquam Vacuum. Legis Jugum. Libertas Evangelii. Du Gloria Intacta.* Below the altar was found the body of *Rosencreuz*, intact, and without any signs of putrefaction. In his hand was a book of parchment, with golden letters marked on the cover with a T(*Testamentum?*), and at the end was written, *Ex Deo naximur. In Jesu morimur. Per Spiritum Sanctum reviviscimus.*" There were signed the names of the brothers present at the funeral of the deceased.

In the year 1615, a new edition of these pamphlets appeared, to which was added another one, entitled *Confessio;* or, "the Confession of the Society and Brotherhood of the R. C.;" giving great promises about future revelations, but ending with the advice to everybody that until these revelations were made the people should continue to believe in the Bible.

All these pamphlets had—as will be shown farther on—one and the same author, and as the *"General Reformation"* was of an entirely satirical character and a pure invention, having no more foundation, in fact, than the *Don Quixote de la Mancha* of *Cervantes*, there is no reason whatever why we should believe that the succeeding pamphlets should have been meant seriously, and that the story of the returned knight, *Christian Rosencreuz*, should have been anything more than an allegory. Moreover, there is no indication of what became of the body of that knight after it was once discovered, nor that the temple of the Holy Ghost (*Sanctus Spiritus*) exists anywhere else but in the hearts of men.

The whole object of these pamphlets seems to have been to present great truths to the ignorant, but to dish them up in a fictitious form, appealing to the curiosity of the people, and to the prevailing craving for a knowledge of the mysteries of Nature, which the majority of the people of these times wanted to know for the purpose of obtaining selfish and personal benefits.

The beauty of the doctrines which shone through these satirical writings were so great and attractive that they excited universal attention; but at the same time the craving of the majority of the people for the mysterious was so great that it blinded their eyes, and rendered them incapable of perceiving the true object of the writer, which was to ridicule the pretensions of dogmatic science and theology, and to draw the people up to a higher conception of true Christianity. The belief in the existence of a real secret organization of Rosicrucians, possessed of the secret how to make gold out of lead and iron, and of prolonging life by means of taking some fluid in the shape of a medicine, was universal; and quacks and pretenders of all kinds roamed over the country and helped to spread the superstitions, often selling worthless compounds for fabulous prices as being the "Elixir of Life;" while others wasted their fortunes and became poor in making vain efforts to transmute metals.

A flood of writings appeared, some attacking and some defending the Rosicrucian Society, which was supposed to exist, but of which no one knew anything. Some people, and even some of the well-informed ones, believed in the existence of such a society; others denied it. But neither one class nor the other could bring any positive proofs for their beliefs. People are always willing to believe that which they desire to be true, and everyone wanted to be admitted as a member of that secret society, of which nobody was certain whether it existed at all; and if anyone boasted of being a Rosicrucian, or succeeded in creating the impression that he was one, he awed the ignorant, and was regarded by them as a very favoured person, and in this way impostors and adventurers often succeeded in preying upon the pockets of the rich.

Those who wanted to be taught magic and sorcery desired that a society or school where they might learn such things should exist; and because they desired it they believed in its existence. If no genuine Rosicrucian could be found, one had to be invented. If the true Rosicrucian society was not to be had, imitations of what was believed to constitute a Rosicrucian society had to be organized. In this way numerous societies were formed, calling themselves "Rosicrucians"; and "Rosicrucianism" took various shapes.

One of the most important publications, and which is calculated to throw light upon the mysterious subject of Rosicrucianism which still perplexes the learned, is the *Chymical Marriage of Christian Rosencreutz*, printed in 1616. This, again, was written to throw ridicule upon the vain and self-conceited dogmatists, scientists, and "gold-makers" of those times, while at the same time it contains high and exalted truths, disguised in an allegorical form, but easily to be perceived by the practical Occultist, *and by him only*. It can easily be seen that the style and tendencies of this publication have a great deal of resemblance to that of the *Fama Fraternitatis*. Now it has been ascertained beyond any doubt that the author of the "Chemical Marriage" was Johann Valentine Andreae,[*] who wrote it while a young

---

[*] *Dr. Johann Velentin Andreae* was born Aug. 17, 1586, at Herrenberg, in Wurtemberg, and died an abbot of Adelsberg, at Stuttgart, June 27, 1654. He spoke several languages, was well versed in theology, mathematics, history, and the natural sciences. He was of a noble mind, anxious to do good, and an original character. Herder describes him as a rose among the thorns.

student in the years 1602 and 1603 in Tübingen. He acknowledges this in the history which he gives of his life, and he adds that he intended to give a true picture of the popular follies of that time. This renders it extremely probable that he was also the author of the "General Reformation," of the *Confessio*, and of the story of Christian Rosencreutz, and this probability amounts to almost conviction if we take into consideration the discovery made afterwards, that the "General Reformation" is nothing else but a literal translation of a part of a book from *Boccalini Ragguagli di Parnaso*. Andreae was a great admirer of that author, and he also adopted his style in his *Mythologia Christiana;* it is therefore plain that he also made the above-named translation, and added it to his "Fama Fraternitatis." Both writings, in fact, form a complement to each other. In the "General Reformation" the political would-be-reformers are held up to ridicule, and in the "Fama" the mystical dreamers, imaginary theosophists, pretended gold-makers, and supposed discoverers of the universal panacea are castigated. There can be no reasonable doubt that this was Andreae's object, and, moreover, his intimate friend, Professor Besoldt, in Tübingen, acknowledged it in saying that the character of both books was plain enough, and that it was very strange that so many intelligent people had been led by the nose to mistake their meaning. Andreae himself, without, however, acknowledging himself to be their author, expressed himself to the effect that the whole was a satire and a fable. In his "confession" he says: (Sc.) *risisse semper Rosicrucianam fabulum et curiositatis fraterculos fuisse in sectatum*† and in his paper entitled *"Turris Babel, seu judiciorum de Fraternitatae Rosaccae crucis chaos,"* he speaks still more plainly upon this subject. It seems to have been his object in this latter publication to help those to become sober again who had become intoxicated by misunderstanding the former publications, for he exclaims: "Listen, ye mortals! In vain will ye wait for the arrival of that fraternity; the comedy is over. The *fama* has played it in, the *fama* has played it out," etc., etc. Still there were many who were not satisfied with this explanation, and who believed that it had been Andreae's intention to cause by his *fama*, a secret society of the scientists of his age to come into existence; but Andreae was too wise to attempt such an absurdity and to apply to the most *unreasonable* persons of his age to form a *reasonable* society.

The question why he should have selected the name "Rosicrucian" for his imaginary society is not difficult to answer. The *Cross* and the *Rose* were favourite symbols among the Alchemists and Theosophists long before anything of a "Rosicrucian Society" was known. Moreover, in his own coat of arms, as in that of Luther, there was a cross and four roses, a circumstance which probably led him to select that name.

---

† Andreae's autobiography. *Weismann*, hist. eccl. P. ii., p. 936.

There is, perhaps, very rarely a fable or work of fiction invented which is not based upon some fact, however disconnected such facts may be with the subject. A work, entitled *Sphinx Rosæa*, printed in 1618, makes it appear very plausible that the writer of the *Fama Fraternitatis*, in inventing the story of *Christian Rosencreutz* and his three brothers, whose number was afterwards increased by four more, had certain originals in his mind, which served as prototypes to construct his story. The author of that *Sphinx* says that the idea of forming such a society for the general reformation of mankind arose from the success of Luther's Reformation; that the knight, Christian Rosencreutz, was, in reality, no other person than a certain *Andreas von Carolstadt*, an adventurer, who had travelled a great deal, but never been in Palestine. He made himself so obnoxious to the clergy of his time, whom he desired to reform, that they, after his death, put the following Epitaph upon his grave:—*Carolstadius Pestis Ecclesiae venonissima, tandem a Diabolo occisus est*. This means: "Here lies Carolstadt, who was a poisonous plague to the Church until the devil killed him at last." The three supposed associates of Rosencreutz were the friends of Carolstadt, the reformer *Zwingli, Oecolompadius,* and *Bucerus,* and the four others, who were supposed to have been added afterwards, were probably *Nicalaus Palargus, Marcus Stubner, Martin Cellurius,* and, finally, *Thomas Münster,* all of which persons were more or less known on account of their desire to aid in reforming the Church.

As the people became infatuated with the idea of becoming Rosicrucians, and no real society of Adepts could be found, they organized Rosicrucian societies without any real Adepts, and thus a great many so-called Rosicrucian societies came into existence. There was one such society founded by *Christian Rose* in 1622, having head centres in the Hague, Amsterdam, Nuremberg, Mantua, Venice, Hamburg, Dantzig and Erfurt. They used to dress in black, and wore at their meetings blue ribbons with a golden wreath and a rose. As a sign of recognition the brothers wore a black silk cord in the top button hole. This ornament was given to the neophytes after they had promised under oath to be strangled by such a cord rather than reveal the secrets which they were supposed to possess. They also had another sign, consisting of the "tonsure," such as is used today by the Roman Catholic clergy, meaning a small round shaven spot on the top of the head, originating probably from the custom of the Buddhist priests, who shave their whole head. Hence many of them wore a wig, in order not to be recognised as belonging to the brotherhood. They led a very quiet life, and were devout people. On all high festivals, very early at sunrise they would leave their residence, and go out through the gate of the town facing the east. When another one of them appeared, or when they met at other places, one would say: *Ave Frater!* to which the other would answer, *Rosae et Aureae;* then the first one said *Crucis,* then both together said: *Benedictus Deus*

Dominus noster, que nobis dedit Signum! They also had for the sake of legitimation a large document, to which the *Imperator* affixed the great seal.*

There was another "Rosicrucian society," formed at Paris in the year 1660 by an apothecary named *Jacob Rose*. This society was dissolved in 1674, in consequence of the notorious case of wholesale poisoning by the ill-reputed Marquise de Brinvillier.

Whether or not there ever were any real Adepts and genuine Alchemists among the members of these Rosicrucian societies, we are, of course, not in a position to affirm. We are satisfied to know that Adepts do exist and that Alchemy is a fact; but whether they had anything to do with these orders we do not know, nor do we care about it, as it is now of no consequence whatever. All that we know for certain in regard to this matter is, that there existed at that time persons in possession of an extraordinary amount of occult knowledge, as is shown by the books they have left; but whether these persons belonged or did not belong to any organized society, is absolutely useless to know.

During the life of *Theophrastus Paracelsus*, he was the intellectual centre to which Alchemists, Occultists, Mystics, Reformers and Rosicrucians were attracted, but there is no indication that he was a member of any society of men calling themselves "Rosicrucians." There is, likewise, no indication that after the time of Paracelsus any organized society of true Adepts, calling themselves "Rosicrucian Society," ever existed. Some of the greatest minds of that age were engaged in occult research, and were naturally attracted together by the bonds of sympathy; but however much they may have been united in the spirit (in the temple of the Holy Ghost), there is no indication that they had an organized society on the external plane, nor would any *real* Adepts need any other but spiritual signs of recognition.

A book printed in 1714, and written by *Sinecrus Renatus*, contains the remarkable information that some years ago the *Masters* of the Rosicrucians had gone to India, and that none of them at present remained in Europe. This is not at all improbable; for the moral atmosphere of Europe is at the present time not very congenial for spirtual development, nor very inviting to those who, while progressing on the Path of Light, are reincarnating in physical forms.

As all researches after a real Rosicrucian society consisting of genuine Adepts were naturally fruitless, the excitement caused by the *Fama Fraternitatis* gradually ceased, and there was not much said or written about them until between the years 1756 and 1768, when a new degree of Freemasonry came into existence, called the "Rosicrucian Knights," or the order of *Rose-croix*, or the *Knights of the Eagle and Pelican;* but we should in vain search among these knights for any genuine Adept, or even for anyone possessed of occult knowledge or

---

* Extracted from the "Sphinx." Vol. I., No. 1.

power; for as our modern churches have lost the key to the mysteries which were once entrusted to their guardianship, and have degenerated into places for social gatherings and religious pastime, so our modern Masons have long ago lost the *Word*, and will not find it again unless they dive below the surface of external ceremonies and seek for it in their own hearts.

The most important books written during the time of the Rosicrucian controversy were the following:—

I. Books Written in Favour of the Rosicrucians:
(Titles translated from the German.)

Fama Fraternitatis, or the discovery of the laudable Order of the Rosy Cross.—*Anonym.*, Frankfurt, 1615.

Confessio, or Confession of the Fraternity of the Rosy Cross.—Anonym., Frankfurt, 1615.

Opinion regarding the laudable Order of the Rosy Cross, by *Adam Bruxius*, M.D., 1616.

Message to the Philosophical Fraternity of the Rosy Cross, by *Valentin Tschirnessus*, Goerlitz.

Thesaurus Fidei, or warning to the novices of the Fraternity of the Rosy Cross, 1619.

Fons Gratiae, by *Trenaeus Agnostus*, C.W., 1619.

Raptus Philosophicus, or Philosophical Revelations for the Fraternity of the R.C., 1619, by *Rhodophilus Stansophorus*.

Silentium Post Clamores. An apology resp. Defence, by *R.M.F.*, 1617.

Frater Crucis Rosacae, or, What kind of people are the Rosicrucians? By *M.A.O.F.W.*, 1617.

Speculum Constantiae. Appeal to new members of the R.C. Society, by *Trenaeus Agnostus*, C.W., 1618.

Themis Aurea. The Laws and Regulations of the laudable Fraternity of the R.C., by *Michael Maier, Imp. Cons. Com. Ey. Ex.*, 1618.

Tintinabulum Sapnorum, or, The Discovery of the blessed Fraternity of the Order of the R.C., by *Trenaeus Agnostus, C.W.*, 1619.

Frater Non Frater. Admonitions to the disciples of the R.C., 1619.

Prodromus Rhodo-Stauroticus. Directions for the practice of Alchemy, 1620.

Colloquium Rhodo-Stauroticum. A discourse regarding the Fraternity of the R.C., 1621.

Rosencreutz Ch. Chemical Marriage, Anno 1459? (1781).

II. Writings Inimical to the Rosicrucians.

Benevolent Advice regarding the Fama and Confessio of the R.C., by *And. Libavius M.D., P.C., Sae. Theolog. and Philosoph.*, 1616.

Sphinx Rosæa. Suspicions in regard to the mysteries of the R.C., by *Christophorus Nigrimus Philomusus and Theologus*, 1618.

The New Arabian and Moorish Fraternity, by *Eusebius Christianus*, a carrier of the wooden cross.

Speculum Ambitionis, or *A Mirror for Ambition*, in which may be seen how the Devil has brought all sorts of new orders into existence. A refutation of the doctrines of that new sect, called Rosicrucians, by *Joh. Hintner*, 1620.

Tomfoolery Discovered, or, Christian Refutation of the so-called Brothers of the Rosy Cross, showing that these people are not of God, but of the Devil. A timely warning to all pious Christians. By *Joh. Silvert Aegl*, 1617.

The more important modern books on Rosicrucianism are: *Semler's* "Collections to the history of the Rosicrucians"; *Bouterwek's* "Origin of the R.C."; *Murr*, "The true origin of Rosicrucians and Freemasons"; *Buhle*, "Origin and history of the R.C."; *Nicolai*, "Remarks about the history of the Rosicrucians and Freemasons"; *Herder*, "An article in the German *Mercury* of March, 1782, and reprinted in Herder's *Philosophy and History*," vol. 15, p. 258; *Arnold*, "History of the churches and heretics," part ii., lib. xvii., cap. 18; *Rossbach*, "Joh. Valentin Andreae and his age," Berlin, 1819. There are numerous books on Alchemy, Theosophy, and Occult Science which have been written by people supposed to have been Rosicrucians; but they give no account of the history of the latter. The most prominent are the works of *Theophrastus Paracelsus, Jacob Boehme, Cornelius Agrippa of Nettesheim; Robert Fludd's* "Summum Bonum"; *John Arndt*, "Silentium Dei," and "The true Christendom"; *Simon Studion*, "Naometria"; *Trenaeus Philalethes*, "Lumen de Lumina," and innumerable others, which may be drawn into this category; but perhaps the most interesting of all is an illustrated work which is now out of print, and has become very rare, and which is entitled *"The Secret Symbols of the Rosicrucians of the Sixteenth and Seventeenth Century,"** and from which a great deal of information contained in this present volume is taken.

---

* This book has been reprinted and published with the fac-similes of the plates by The Aries Press, Chicago, Ill.

Vade retro satanas. Nunquam mihi suade vana. Sunt mala quæ libas. Ipse venena bibas.

Chapter Six.

PSEUDO-ROSICRUCIANS—IMPOSTORS AND FOOLS.

The fool's paradise is the world of self-created illusions, without the recognition of the underlying eternal truth.

THE Devil is God inverted. Falsehood is truth perverted. The spirit produces the form to be its true image; but, for all that the form does not always represent the true qualities of the spirit. Thus the sun shines upon the earth, and his rays produce wholesome and poisonous growths, and the spirit of Christ for ever remains in His glory, even if a thousand of so-called "Christian" sects misrepresent Him, so that His image can no more be recognised in them. Likewise the true Brothers of the Golden and Rosy Cross still exist, even if the name of their order has been misused by impostors and fools.

The age at which the idea of Rosicrucian societies became popular was a time when orders of all kinds were flourishing. Monasteries, convents, and religious orders were the plagues of the country; in some places the Catholic clergy, in others the Protestant clergy, were, so to say, omnipotent. The work of the great Reformation had only begun its work, and free thought and free speech were little known. The Protestant clergy were not less intolerant than the Catholics who preceded them, and in some places the latter were still in possession of all the authority they possessed at the time of the Inquisition.

In consequence of the power of the Church over the citizens of the country—a power which the former abused very freely—it became necessary to have secret societies and places where the members could secretly meet and exchange thir opinions without being overheard by spies and traitors. Secret orders of all kinds were, therefore, existing in great numbers, and foremost of all were the *Freemasons,* an order which, on account of the strength of its principles, has continued to exist. At that time Masonry was not what it is now. A writer of those times, in a work published in 1666, informs us that it was neither a political nor a Christian institution, but a truly secret organization, which admitted such men as members who were anxious to obtain the priceless boon of liberty of conscience, and to avoid clerical prosecution.

But the air of mystery which hung about the masonic lodges was also very attractive to all who were mystically inclined. Then, as now, strange rumours circulated about the doings of the Masons, wild stories were whispered about among the ignorant, which the clergy of those times, like their brothers of the present day, helped to start, circulate, and exaggerate. They were accused of practising black magic and sorcery, and some even accused them of being in league with devils.

All these things served to attract to the masonic lodges not merely those who were desirous of freedom of speech, but also those who desired to learn forbidden secrets; and, moreover, adventurers of all kinds sought to gain admittance and sometimes succeeded. Many of the masonic brothers attempted to study and practise alchemy; and there are some accounts proving that sometimes successful alchemical experiments were made in the lodges. But, generally speaking, then, as now, those who joined a lodge for the purpose of having some very important secrets revealed to them, were sadly disappointed, for besides the external ceremonies and forms, which they were sworn not to reveal, and which were of no further importance, they were informed of nothing which would have been worth revealing. They went from one degree to another, paying large sums for being admitted into higher degrees, and still no revelations were made, and all they learned on such occasions was some other form of ceremony, a knowledge of which was hardly worth the price they paid for it.

It is, therefore, not surprising that when the Rosicrucian mania broke out, and when the more exaggerated accounts about the great powers of that order were fully believed, that the Masons opened their ranks to anyone who was supposed to be a Rosicrucian, and that if the latter succeeded in making the brothers believe that he was actually such a favoured person, he would at once gain a great deal of influence in the lodge. These circumstances opened the doors of the masonic lodges to a great many strolling adventurers, vagabonds, charlatans, and mountebanks; and especially the Catholic as well as the Protestant "Jesuits" were not slow to see their advantage, and to gain admission to the lodges under the disguise of Rosicrucians.

They pretended to be in communication with certan unknown superiors, some grand patriarch of Jerusalem, or some invisible somebody, whose orders had to be obeyed without asking any questions, but whose names must not be revealed; and to make such supposed orders more effective, they produced letters and documents apparently coming from such superiors, but which they had written and sealed themselves. On some occasions they performed sleight-of-hand tricks, produced sham apparitions of ghosts and deceased persons, for the purpose of deluding the members of the lodge, and to make them believe in their supernatural powers. Thus they made Freemasonry their tool and used the power which they gained for the advancement of their own interests.

Volumes might be filled with amusing accounts of the doings of the pseudo-Rosicrucians; but we have only room for a few examples, and shall, for that purpose, select those whose influence in history was of considerable importance.

One of the adventurers, of whom it is still doubtful whether or not he possessed any occult powers, was the reputed *Schroepfer*, a bankrupt inn-keeper of Leipzig. His only object seemed to be to make as much money as he could, and to spend it as fast he made it. He assumed the name "von Steinbach," and pretended to be a French Colonel, and to have been appointed by the Duke of Orleans as secret ambassador, sent to reform masonry, and to establish a connection with the Jesuits, who were at that time driven away. These Jesuits, he said, were in possession of an enormous amount of treasure, which they had entrusted to his care; but his intention was to use that money for the benefit of the country, and whoever wanted to obtain a share of it would have to come to confession and to better his life.

It is almost incredible that any sane person should have believed such nonsense; nevertheless, when a prospect of obtaining money is held out, most people are ready to believe almost anything. Moreover, Schroepfer had a wonderful power of gaining the confidence of those who came near him, and he had some knowledge of chemistry, which gave him a scientific air, and so it happened that even some people of high social position believed in his assertions.

To gain full power over his dupes, he deposited in a bank at Frankfurt a sealed package, to be returned to him whenever he desired it; this package was said to contain several millions in bank-notes, but which, as might have been supposed, contained nothing but brown paper. On the strength of that supposed deposit, which "could not then be touched," he borrowed large sums of money. He even gained the confidence of the Duke of *Cairland*, in whose presence he caused the apparition of the *Chevalier de Saxe* to appear in the palace. This scene is described by an eye-witness as follows:—"The large room wherein the ghost was to appear had the form of a theatre, and had formerly been used for the purpose of giving private plays and operas. The spectators were sitting in a half-circle, and they received strict orders not to leave their seats under any circumstances, nor to touch nor examine any of the apparatus for the conjuring process, else the most dread consequences would follow. They had, furthermore, to swear that they would not reveal afterwards what they had seen.

The Duke and his Minister, von Wurmb, and other dignitaries were present. Schroepfer appeared, nodded to the assembly, and walked in a haughty manner up to the platform. The Duke had desired to see the apparition of the Chevalier de Saxe, and Schroepfer consented. Suddenly all the candles in the room went out at once, and every one present felt a feeling of horror creeping over him. At the same time a stupefying smoke of some incense which Schroepfer was burning filled the room. Gradually the platform grew more light, while the place for the spectators remained in darkness. A kind of bluish light shone upon the faces of the latter, which gave to every one of them a ghostly appearance. Gradually a cloud became visible in the background of the stage. At first it was only like a thin mist, but slowly it grew more solid. Gradually it assumed the outlines of a human form. The details of the figure became clearer, the face could be seen and recognised; there was the living image of the Chevalier de Saxe.

"The Duke, seeing his dead relative standing before him, broke out in an exclamation of horror. The apparition lifted its arm. Every one was terrified; none dared to speak. There were deep sighs.

"Then the ghost began to speak in a hollow voice, complaining that he had been disturbed in his sleep in the grave.

"The Duke appeared to be near fainting; but being a courageous man, he rose with an effort, and it seemed for a moment that his reason was to be victorious over superstition.

"Laying his hand on his sword, he exclaimed, 'Illusion of hell! Go back to the place from whence you came!'

"At that moment the sword dropped from his hand, as if he had been suddenly paralyzed. The apparition was gone and the room was dark. Suddenly, as quickly as they had been extinguished, the candles began to burn again, and we all saw the conjuror in his long habit of black velvet, looking still paler than usual, the sweat standing upon his forehead, resembling a man who has just escaped some great danger. Having recovered, he turned to the Duke and reproached him.

"'Your Excellency,' said Schroepfer, 'may congratulate yourself that we have not all been killed. Only the most powerful conjurations on my part could prevent the apparition from murdering us. It was the most terrible hour of my life.'

"The Duke excused himself, and finally begged pardon, promising to be more obedient at some future occasion."

"There were a great many people of whom Schroepfer had borrowed money, sometimes even large sums, and they all grew impatient, and wanted to be paid. Schroepfer was forced to produce the package from the bank, and it was found to be worthless. But even that was not sufficient to destroy the confidence of his dupes. They persuaded themselves that he was a high Rosicrucian Adept, who was only testing their faith. "Can we, in our ignorance," they said, "head the Master's heart and know his intentions? Perhaps he is going to take away our earthly Mammon, and give us for it the imperishable philosopher's stone."

"At last, however, the measure was full; the creditors refused to be fed any longer on idle promises; they wanted their money. So they selected a deputation from their midst, and sent them to Leipzig, where Schroepfer had gone to escape their importunity. When they entered his room he bade them welcome in a kind manner and full of assurance.

"I have already been informed of your coming," he said, "and have been waiting for you."

"Then," they answered, "you will also know that we have come for the purpose of obtaining a settlement of our financial affairs."

"What!" exclaimed Schroepfer, appearing to be astonished, "do you doubt me?'

"Not I," answered the one addressed; "but some of my friends do."

"And you, sir?" asked Schroepfer, turning to another one and fixing his eyes upon him.

The person addressed trembled, and began to stammer an excuse; but Schroepfer, whose face assumed a triumphant smile, continued:—

"Oh, you of little faith! ye are worse than the doubting Thomas, more obstinate than Peter, who thrice denied his Master. I have opened before you the portals of the spirit world and made you see its inhabitants, and you still doubt my power. I wanted to lead you into the innermost sanctuary, and to make you richer than all the kings of this earth; but you have not stood the test imposed upon you. Shame upon you! Without faith and confidence no miracle can be performed. Doubt is the great sin of the world."

"Mercy, great master!" exclaimed one; "do not punish the innocent with the guilty. I did not doubt."

"I know it," answered Schroepfer; "and for the sake of one just man, I will forgive the sins of all. The mammon after which your sinful heart hankers, you shall receive; what I promised will be done; but it would have been better for you if you had chosen the hidden wisdom instead of possessions which perish."

They then begged his pardon, and at last he became less stern and forgave them their doubts. He promised not only to unveil to them all the secrets of the true Rosicrucians, but he also appointed a certain day for the payment of his debt.

The revelations about the secrets never came; but the day appointed for the payment of the debt arrived. In the evening preceding that eventful day, Schroepfer invited all his creditors to his house. The supper which was served was excellent, the wine of the first quality. Schroepfer was in high spirits, more talkative than usual, and amused his guests by some clever sleight-of-hand tricks, attributing it, of course, all to the spirits. Midnight passed, and the guests prepared themselves to depart for their residences, but the host objected.

"I shall not let you go," he said, "you may all sleep here, and in the morning, even before sunrise, I will show you something entirely new. Heretofore I have shown you dead people whom I have called back into life; but this morning I will show you a living man whom you will believe to be dead." He then took up his glass filled with wine, and caused it to jingle by bringing it in contact with the glasses held by the others, with each one successively. As he approached the last one, his glass broke into pieces.

"What does this mean?" asked one.

"The fate of mankind," answered Schroepfer. "The wine of life has escaped, the vessel broke to pieces; I am fatigued enough to die."

He feel asleep, and the guests followed his example, sleeping in armchairs and on lounges as well as they could manage it. Early in the morning Schroepfer called to them to awake; telling them that it was time to go. They all went together out of the town to an almost solitary place called the "Rosenthal." Schroepfer was silent, and appeared to be very serious. Having arrived at the place of destination, he ordered his companions to remain where he posted them.

"Do not move," he said, "until I call you to help me to raise the buried treasure. I am now going into that grove, where you will soon see a wonderful apparition."

With a satirical smile on his pale face he turned away and disappeared in the bushes. Soon a sound as of a pistol-shot sounded from there. They thought that it was perhaps fired by some hunter, and paid no further attention to it. They waited. One quarter of an hour after another passed away, and nothing happened. They did not dare to leave their places, fearing to rouse the anger of the magician by their disobedience. The mist of the morning had turned into a fine rain, which made their position very uncomfortable. They grew impatient, and consulted with each other what was to be done. While they were discussing the subject, some proposing to follow Shroepfer into the bushes, and others objecting, saying that by doing so they might interrupt his incantations, or at least give him a welcome excuse for not obtaining the treasure, a stranger approached. His appearance was so sudden that it almost appeared miraculous.

"I know," said the stranger, "for whom you are waiting. Schroepfer will not come; he is dead."

"You lie!" exclaimed one of the company, being very indignant about this intrusion.

Instead of answering, the stranger gave a certain secret sign which proved him to be one of the superiors of a high masonic order. All present bowed respectfully.

"Follow me," he said, "and you will see that I told you the truth."

They followed him into the ticket, and there they found the magician dead upon the sod. He held a pistol in his hand; the ball had penetrated his heart.

Thus perished a man who, although he was an impostor, may nevertheless have been in possession of some occult knowledge, but who had not strength enough to resist the temptations of the senses, and who misused his powers for the gratification of his personal self.

Johann Christoph Woellner was the son of a Protestant clergyman, who resided near Spandau, and became preacher of the Evangelical community at Grossbehnitz, near Berlin. While in this position he succeeded in seducing the daughter of his patron, the General Itzenplitz, and the family at last consented to a marriage which they could not prevent. The affair was still more scandalous on account of the publicly known fact that Woellner made love to the mother of the girl before he married the latter. By this marriage he acquired a considerable fortune. He was very much inclined to mysticism, and soon became one of the most active and prominent members of the Rosicrucians. His name in the lodge was *Chrysophron*, and by the influence of his friends he obtained an influential position, which he used for the advancement of his own selfish interests, and finally he obtained a position at the Prussian Court.

He appeared externally very modest and meek; while at the same time his conceit and ambition were without limits, and no means were too vile to him, if by them he could accomplish his purpose. His low forehead indicated a person of very little intelligence, but a great deal of cunning. His little eyes were continually looking downwards; his manners were those of a pious coxcomb. Sympathetic souls find each other, and he therefore became very intimate with *Bischofswerder*, another pseudo-Rosicrucian, who was Minister of State and favourite of King Frederic William II. of Prussia, and he in company with his friend worked together for the destruction of the religious liberty of the people, as shall be described further on.

Another of the same class was the pastor *Johann August Stark*, an Evangelical preacher, but secretly a Catholic, and in league with the Jesuits. He was an extraordinary hypocrite. Still worse, but more ridiculous, was his disciple, the pseudo-Rosicrucian *Mayr*, a very eccentric character and a great fanatic. He was limping, bald-headed, squinted, and of most unprepossessing appearance. A broad trunk, with an immense hydrocephalic head rested upon thin, weak legs. He usually wore black pantaloons and vest, and an orange-coloured coat. While preaching, he shot with a pistol from the pulpit at a man who slept during the sermon, and wounded him, exclaiming, "I will wake you up!" He had all kinds of religions. In the morning he went to the Catholic mass, next he preached in the Protestant church, then spent his afternoons in the Jewish synagogue or with the Mennonites, and in the evening he went to the masonic lodge.

These were some of the types of the "Rosicrucians" which infested the masonic lodges of those times, and it is a marvel that they did not destroy masonry. Some of them were impostors, others were dupes, and not a few imposed upon their dupes, while at the same time they were the dupes of others. This confusion of incompatible elements, such as freethinkers, pietists, reasonable men, and superstitious fools, could not fail to bring on a separation within the lodges, and they naturally became divided into two parts, of which one represented progression and tolerance, the other one bigotry and superstition. Among the latter class was the "Society of the Cross," who at their initiation had to take the following oath: "In the name of the crucified I swear to break all ties which bind me to my father, mother, brothers, sisters, wife, relatives, friends, sweethearts, king, benefactors, or to any other human being, whom I may have sworn to obey, so that I may belong entirely to Christ."

The Crown Prince, afterwards King Frederic William II. of Prussia, was himself a member of a masonic lodge and a great admirer of Woellner and Bischofswerder, who exerted their nefarious influence over him, and whenever the unfortunate prince appeared to become subject to doubts regarding the supernatural powers of his friends, they quieted him again by causing the spectre of some dead friend to appear before him, which was not at all difficult to do, as they were in possession of all the paraphernalia necessary to perform sleight-of-hand tricks, such as magic lanterns, electric batteries, etc.; and there was no danger of being detected in these tricks, as the spectators had to remain within a certain "magic" circle, which they were not permitted to leave; and it was always said that a disobedience to the orders of the magician would be followed by the direst consequences, or perhaps be fatal to all.

The greatest enemies of the so-called *"Rosicrucians"* were the *Illuminati*, a secret organization, radiating throughout the whole of Germany. At their head stood the councillor *Weishaupt*, formerly professor at the University of Ingolstadt, in Bavaria. He had been educated in his youth in a Jesuit convent, but afterwards became a bitter enemy of that order. He wanted to liberate the people from the bonds of bigotry by spreading his cosmopolitan ideas, and he founded the order of the *Illuminati*, using the already existing masonic symbols and formulæ. He proclaimed that the object of his order was not to interfere with the Church or State, but that it intended to work for the moral improvement of humanity, to do good, to prevent evil, and to spread useful knowledge to all parts of the world. The necessary requirements to become a member of his order are described by him as follows:—

"He who is not deaf to the voice of suffering, whose heart is open to charity, and who is the brother and friend of the unfortunate, is our brother. He should love all creatures, and not cause pain even to a worm. He ought to be constant in adversity, indefatigable in doing good, courageous in overcoming difficulties. He should not look with contempt upon the weak; he should be above all selfish and personal considerations, and be anxious to benefit mankind. He should avoid idleness, and not consider any kind of knowledge to be below his dignity to investigate. But the main object of his life should be the attainment of self-knowledge. He who cares for virtue and truth for its own sake will not care for the applause of the vulgar. He who dares to do that which his own heart commands him to do is fit to become a member of our order."

His order, like all secret orders, possessed the charm which always surrounds that which is mysterious. It had three degrees; the first one consisted of the *novices* and the *minervales*. After passing an examination, the candidate was accepted into a higher degree, consisting of the *lesser* and the *higher* degree of *Illuminati*, and finally followed the highest degree, the *Priests*. According to Weishaupt's ideas, the main object of true religion was to lift man up to a higher conception of his true nature and destiny, and thereby bring him up to a realization of this higher state of human dignity. This could not be accomplished by force, but merely by the spreading of knowledge, displacing error and superstition. He thought that if men could once realize the necessity of virtue and be all united by brotherly love, immorality, vice, degradation, and poverty would cease to exist, and men would become their own rulers and guides.

He furthermore attempted to prove that true (esoteric) Christianity was not a popular religion, or a religion for the vulgar, but that it was a system of philosophy, given in symbols, comprehensible only to those who were far enough advanced to be instructed in it, and it was the duty of the Illuminati to study the esoteric side of the religious systems, and to try to comprehend their meaning.

The highest rank in the highest degree was that of *Regent*. The Regents were the superiors of the order, and only the most useful and virtuous members were admitted to that rank, after having passed through long and severe probations.*

Soon the *Illuminati* became objects of fear and suspicion for the Governments, especially in Bavaria. A Protestant clergyman, *Lange*, was accidentally killed by a stroke of lightning. When his body was examined by the authorities, they found some papers regarding the order, and a list of some of its prominent members. This was the signal for a universal inquisition and persecution. Many of the noblest and most eminent persons were imprisoned or banished, others fled, and a price was set upon Weishapt's head, who, however, escaped to *Gotha*, where he found an asylum.†

Still the order of the *Illuminati* continued to exist, and between them and the *Rosicrucians* there existed the same animosity as now between the *Liberals* and the *Ultramontanes,* or between Progressionists and Conservatives. Each party denounced the other one, and each party had some just cause; for the Rosicrucians attempted to push the people still lower into darkness and superstition, while the Illuminati

---

* See *Weishaupt*, "Intercourse with Man."

† This took place in the year 1758, under the reign of *Maximillian Joseph*, who has been called *The Beloved* on account of his goodness. The doctrines of Weishaupt were none other than the doctrines of Christ; but they were not in conformity with the personal interests of autocratic "Christian" priests, who have ever been the real enemies of the truth and light, and the servants of darkness and evil.

gave them a light which the people did not understand, and by undermining the authority of the priesthood, which governed the people by fear, they also undermined the authority of the law, by which the people must be ruled, as long as they cannot rule themselves.

King Frederic the Great cared nothing about these religious quarrels. In his dominions everyone was at liberty to follow the religion which suited him best; and all the efforts of the Rosicrucians were therefore directed to maintain their power over the Crown Prince, and in this they succeeded. The Crown Prince was a good-hearted but weakminded man, whose strength had been to a certain extent exhausted by too much sensual enjoyment. He often had spells of great moral depression and brooded over his regrets for the past. He needed some comfort and consolation, and this he attempted to find sometimes in the arms of the Countess of Lichtenau; at other times in those of the pietists and "Rosicrucians," *Bischofswerder* and *Woellner*.

These "Rosicrucians" used all the means they could to obtain power. They calumniated Frederic the Great, and saw in him their greatest enemy, because his liberal measures hindered them from forcing their narrow-minded ideas and bigotry upon the people. They frightened the credulous Crown Prince by painting and exaggerating to him the dire consequences of the spreading of "irreligious" doctrines. They proposed to restore the Inquisition in a Protestant shape.

Frederic the Great died; *Frederic William II.* became King; but he was ruled by Bischofswerder and Woellner, and by his mistresses. One of the first successful attempts of the former was to restore to a great extent the power of *Rome* in Protestant Germany. Woellner became Minister of the religious department, and soon followed the issue of the infamous *"religious edict"* of July 9, 1788. In this edict everybody was warned by order of the King to subordinate his own reason to the dogmas of the Church; and those who should contravene this order were theatened with the loss of the offices they held and with imprisonment. They generously permitted everybody to believe what he pleased, but they strongly prohibited any expression of opinion in regard to religious matters, if such opinions were not sanctioned by the Church. But those who should dare to ridicule a clergyman were threatened with the heaviest punishment. At the same time *censure* was established, so that nothing could be printed and published without having first been submitted to the clerical authorities for approval.

The excitement caused by this shameful edict was terrible. The Illuminati led by the bookseller *Nicolay*, at Berlin, protested against it; but their writings were confiscated. Woellner surrounded himself with "Rosicrucians" and pietists and a "spiritual examination board" was instituted, which examined every candidate for an office in regard to his creed before he could be appointed. They examined all clergymen and school teachers and ejected everyone who was not a hypocrite and who dared to say what he thought. They published a miserable catechism written in bad Latin, in which was prescribed what a person would have to believe before he could pass the examination. Pietistic schools and hymn-books were introduced and everything possible was attempted to make the people more stupid than they already were.

The disgrace which was brought upon the name "Rosicrucians" by these *pseudo-Rosicrucians* was so great that even to this day everything connected with Rosicrucianism is believed by the public in Germany to be identical with bigotry, pietism, hypocrisy, knavery, animalism, and absurdity.

APPENDIX.

THE PRINCIPLES
OF THE
YOGA-PHILOSOPHY
OF THE
ROSICRUCIANS AND ALCHEMISTS.

The following pages were originally intended to form the basis of a separate work, entitled *"A Key to the Secret Symbols of the Rosicrucians."* As the idea of bringing out such a book has been abandoned for the present, they have been added as a suitable appendix to the foregoing historical notes.

It will be found that the doctrines presented herein contain the most profound secrets, especially in regard to the "resurrection of the flesh." They go to show that the physical body is neither a useless nor a despicable thing, and that Matter is as necessary to Spirit, as Spirit to Matter. Without the presence of a living body no resurrection could take place; neither could the Spirit have any relative existence without the presence of a material form. The state of Nirvana is not to be attained by merely dreaming about it, and before Man can rise superior to anything he must have attained that to which he desires to become superior. Only from the soul resurrected within the body of flesh arises the glorified spirit.

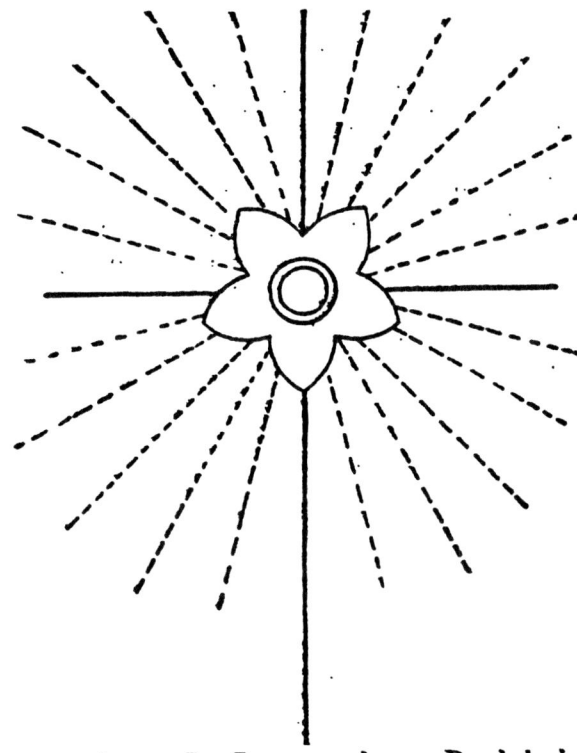

Ex Deo nascimur. In Jesu morimur. Reviviscimus per Spiritum Sanctum.

Chapter Seven

IN THE PRONAOS OF THE TEMPLE OF THE TRUE ROSY CROSS.

Our salvation is the life of Christ in us.

THE place or *state* wherein the true Rosicrucian lives is far too exalted and glorious to be described in words. When we enter the vestibule of the temple of the true Rosy Cross, we enter into a region of unalloyed bliss and happiness. There is an effulgence of super-terrestrial light, where all aborious thinking and exercise of the imagination for the purpose of drawing logical inferences about the unknown, ceases, for in that light is the realm of pure knowledge; to live there is to perceive, and to perceive is to know. Into that paradise of celestial consciousness nothing impure can enter. No room is there for terrestrial flesh and blood; but the spiritual beings which inhabit that realm are made of the flesh and body of "Christ," in other words, of the substance of the spiritual soul.

H. P. Blavatsky, in her "Key to Theosophy," says that there are beings having attained a state of spiritual consciousness which would entitle them to enter the state of Nirvana; nevertheless, out of compassion for mankind, they still remain residents of this earth, inhabiting invisibly for mortal eyes the astral plane of our planet. In that, she describes the true order of the *Golden and Rosy Cross* as a spiritual

Brotherhood, and if one of these superior beings, for some purpose or other, reincarnates in a human body upon this planet, then will there be a real Rosicrucian in a visible form upon this earth.

The "history" of that "brotherhood" is the history of the evolution of the world, and that of the spiritual regeneration of the soul and the body of man; for although each of these individual beings had its own terrestial history and experiences in passing through many incarnations upon this planet, nevertheless, in its essential points the history of all is alike, and consisted in the conquering of the low and the unfoldment of the high. They all had to bear the *Cross* of suffering before they could become crowned with victory; they all had to crucify their selfish and personal will, and die in regard to all that attracts the soul to the sphere of earthly desires and illusions before they could have the spiritual faculties of their souls unfolded like the *Rose* whose leaves are unfolded by the rays of the rising sun.

ROSICRUCIAN RULES.

1. Love God above all.

To "love God" means to love wisdom and truth. We can love God in no other way than in being obedient to Divine law; and to enable us to exercise that obedience conscientiously requires knowledge of the law, which can only be gained by practice.

2. Devote your time to your spiritual advancement.

As the sun without leaving his place in the sky sends his rays upon the earth to shine upon the pure and the impure, and to illuminate even the most minute material objects with his light; likewise the spirit of man may send his mental rays into matter to obtain knowledge of all terrestrial things; but there is no need that the spirit should thereby lose its own divine self-consciousness, and be itself absorbed by the objects of its perception.

3. Be entirely unselfish.

Spiritual knowledge begins only where all sense of self ceases. Where the delusion which causes man to imagine himself to be a being separated and isolated from others ends, there he begins to realize his true state as an all-embracing universal and divine self-conscious power.

4. Be temperate, modest, energetic, and silent.

The door to the inner temple is called "Contentment"; but no animal can enter therein, only he who walks uprightly, being conscious of his true dignity as a human being. Without energy, nothing can be accomplished; and only in the silence, when all thoughts and desires are at rest, can the Divine harmonies penetrate to the internal ear.

5. Learn to know the origin of the METALS *contained within thyself.*

Ignorance is the cause of suffering. That which is material must be crucified and die, so that that which is spiritual may be resurrected and live.

6. *Beware of quacks and pretenders.*

He who claims to be in possession of knowledge knows nothing; only he through whom the Word of wisdom speaks is wise.

7. *Live in constant adoration of the highest good.*

The worm seeks for pleasure among abomination and filth; but the free eagle spreads his wings and rises up towards the sun.

8. *Learn the theory before you attempt the practice.*

He who travels with a trustworthy guide will be safer than he who refuses to profit by the experience of another.

9. *Exercise charity towards all beings.*

All beings are one in the spirit; divided from each other merely by the illusion of form. He who is charitable towards another form in which the universal One Life is manifest, saves suffering to his own self.

10. *Read the ancient books of wisdom.*

Books are to the unripe mind that which the mother's milk is to the nursling. We must receive drink from others until we have gained sufficient strength and experience to descend to the living fountain within ourselves, and to draw from there the water of truth.

11. *Try to understand their secret meaning.*

That which is external may be seen with the external eye; but that which is spiritual can only be seen with the eye of the spirit.

These are the eleven rules which ought to be followed by those who desire to enter the temple of the Rosy Cross; but the Rosicrucians have a twelfth rule, an *Arcanum*, in which great powers reside, but of which it is not lawful to speak. This Arcanum will be given to those who deserve it, and by its aid they will find light in the darkness, and a guiding hand through the labyrinth. This Arcanum is inexpressible in the language of mortals, and it can, therefore, only be communicated from *heart to heart*. There is no torture strong enough to extract it from the true Rosicrucian; for even if he were willing to reveal it, those who are unworthy of it are not capable of receiving it.

THE DUTIES OF A ROSICRUCIAN.

Those who are dead in the flesh will read the following with the external understanding; those who live in the spirit will see its internal meaning, and act accordingly.

The duties of a true Rosicrucian are:—

1. *To alleviate suffering and to cure the sick without accepting any remuneration.*

The medicine which they give is more valuable than gold; it is of an invisible kind, and can be had for nothing everywhere.

2. *To adopt the style of their clothing to the costumes of the country wherein they reside for the time being.*

The clothing of the spirit is the form which he inhabits, and must be adapted to the conditions of the planet whereon he resides.

3. To meet once a year in a certain place.

Those who do not meet at that place, when their terrestrial career is over will have their names taken out of the book of life.

4. Each member has to select a proper person to be his successor.

Each man is himself the creator of that being whose personality he adopts on the next step on the ladder of evolution.

5. The letters R.C. are the emblem of the order.

Those who have truly entered the order will bear the marks upon their body, which cannot be mistaken by him who is capable of recognising them.

6. The existence of the Brotherhood is to be kept secret for one hundred years, beginning from the time when it was first established.

Nor will the "hundred years" be over until man has awakened to the consciousness of his own divine nature.

THE SECRET SIGNS OF THE ROSICRUCIANS.

There are sixteen signs by which a member of the order of the Rosicrucians may be known. He who possesses only a few of those signs is not a member of a very high degree, for the true Rosicrucian possesses them all.

1. The Rosicrucian is Patient.

His first and most important victory is the conquest of his own self. It is the victory over the LION, who has bitterly injured some of the best followers of the Holy Cross. He is not to be vanquished by a fierce and inconsiderate attack made upon him; but he must be made to surrender to patience and fortitude. The true Rosicrucian tries to overcome his enemies by kindness, and those who hate him by gifts. He heaps not curses, but the burning fire of love upon their heads. He does not persecute his enemies with the sword, or with faggots, but he suffers the weeds to grow with the wheat until they are both matured, when they will be separated by Nature.

2. The Rosicrucian is Kind.

He never appears gloomy or melancholy, or with a scowl or sneer upon his face. He acts kindly and politely towards everybody, and is always ready to render assistance to others. Although he is different from the majority of other people, still he tries to accommodate himself to their ways, habits and manners, as much as his dignity will permit. He is, therefore, an agreeable companion, and knows how to converse with the rich as well as with the poor, and to move among all classes of society so as to command their respect; for he has conquered the bear of vulgarity.

3. The Rosicrucian knows no Envy.

Before he is accepted into the order he must go through the terrible ordeal of cutting off the head of the snake of envy; which is a very difficult labour, because the snake is sly, and easily hides itself in some corner. The true Rosicrucian is always content with his lot, knowing that it is such as he deserves it to be. He never worries about the advantages or riches which others possess, but wishes always the best to everybody. He knows that he will obtain all he deserves, and he cares not if any other person possesses more than he. He expects no favours, but he distributes his favours without any partiality.

4. *The Rosicrucian does not Boast.*

He knows that man is nothing but an instrument in the hands of GOD, and that he can accomplish nothing useful by his own will; the latter being nothing but the will of GOD perverted in man. To GOD he gives all the praise, and to that which is mortal he gives all the blame. He is in no inordinate haste to accomplish a thing, but he waits until he receives his orders from the Master who resides above and within. He is careful what he speaks about, and uses no unhallowed language.

5. *The Rosicrucian is not Vain.*

He proves thereby that there is something real in him, and that he is not like a blown-up bag filled with air. Applause or blame leaves him unaffected, nor does he feel aggrieved if he is contradicted or encounters contempt. He lives within himself, and enjoys the beauties of his own inner world, but he never desires to show off his possessions, nor to pride himself on any spiritual gifts which he may have attained. The greater his gifts, the greater will be his modesty, and the more will he be willing to be obedient to the law.

6. *The Rosicrucian is not Disorderly.*

He always strives to do his duty, and to act according to the order established by the law. He cares nothing for externalities, nor for ceremonies. The law is written within his heart, and therefore all his thoughts and acts are ruled by it. His respectability is not centred in his external appearance, but in his real being, which may be compared to a root from which all his actions spring. The interior beauty of his soul is reflected upon his exterior, and stamps all his acts with its seal; the light existing in his heart may be perceived in his eye by an expert; it is the mirror of the Divine image within.

7. *The Rosicrucian is not Ambitious.*

There is nothing more injurious to spiritual development and expansion of the soul than a narrow mind and a selfish character. The true Rosicrucian always cares much more for the welfare of others than for his own. He has no private or personal interest to defend or foster. He always seeks to do good, and he never avoids any opportunity which may present itself for that purpose.

8. *The Rosicrucian is not Irritable.*

It is evident that a person who works for the benefit of the whole will be hated by those whose personal advantages are not benefited thereby; because selfishness is opposed to magnanimity, and the claims of the few are not always compatible with the interests of the community. The Rosicrucian will therefore be often resisted by narrow-minded and short-sighted people; he will be slandered by calumniators, his motives will be misrepresented, he will be misjudged by the ignorant, ridiculed by the would-be wise, and taunted by the fool. All such proceedings, however, cannot excite or irritate the mind of the true Rosicrucian, nor disturb the divine harmony of his soul; for his faith rests in the perception and knowledge of the truth within himself. The opposition of a thousand ignorant people will not induce him to desist from doing that which he knows to be noble and good, and he will do it even if it should involve the loss of his fortune or of his life. Being able and accustomed to direct his spiritual sight towards the divine, he cannot be deluded by the illusions of matter, but clings to the eternal reality. Being surrounded by angelic influences, and listening to their voices, he is not affected by the noise made by the animals. He lives in the company of those noble beings, who were once men like others, but who have become transfigured, and who are now beyond the reach of the vulgar and low.

9. *The Rosicrucian does not think evil of others.*

Those who think evil of others see merely the evil which exists within themselves reflected and mirrored forth in others. The Rosicrucian is always willing to recognise in everything that which is good. Tolerance is a virtue by which the Rosicrucian is eminently distinguished from others; and by which he may be known. If a thing appears to be ambiguous, he suspends his judgment about it until he has investigated its nature; but as long as his judgment is not perfect, he is more inclined to form a good opinion than an evil one about everything.

10. *The Rosicrucian loves justice.*

He, however, never sets himself up as a judge over the faults of others, nor does he wish to appear to be wise by censuring the mistakes of others. He does not enjoy gossip, and cares no more about the foolishness committed by others, than he would about the buzzing of a fly or the capers of a monkey. He finds no pleasure in listening to political or personal quarrels, disputations, or mutual recriminations. He cares nothing for the cunningness of a fox, the dissimulation of a crocodile, or the rapacity of a wolf, and is not amused by the stirring up of mud. His nobility of character lifts him up into a sphere far beyond all such trifles and absurdities, and being above the sensual plane, wherein ordinary mortals find their happiness and enjoyment, he lives with those who do not think evil of each other, who do not rejoice about an injustice done to their brother, or make merry about his ignorance, and enjoy his misfortunes. He enjoys the company of those who love the truth, and who are surrounded by the peace and harmony of the spirit.

11. *The Rosicrucian loves the truth.*

There is no devil worse than falsehood and calumny. Ignorance is a nonentity, but falsehood is the substance of evil. The calumniator rejoices whenever he has found something upon which to base his lies and to make them grow like mountains. Opposed to it is the truth, it being a ray of light from the eternal fountain of GOOD, which has the power to transform man into a divine being. The ROSICRUCIAN seeks, therefore, no other light but the light of truth, and this light he does not enjoy alone, but in company of all who are good and filled with its divine majesty, whether they live on this earth or in the spiritual state; and he enjoys it above all with those who are persecuted, oppressed, and innocent, but who will be saved by the truth.

12. *The Rosicrucian knows how to be silent.*

Those who are false do not love the truth. Those who are foolish do not love wisdom. The true Rosicrucian prefers to enjoy the company of those who can appreciate truth to that of those who would trample it with their feet. He will keep that which he knows locked up within his heart, for in silence is power. As a minister of state does not go about telling to everybody the secrets of the king; so the Rosicrucian does not parade before the public the revelations made to him by the king within, who is nobler and wiser than all the earthly kings and princes; for they only rule by the authority and power derived from Him. His secrecy ceases only when the king commands him to speak, for it is then not he who speaks, but the truth that is speaking through him.

13. *The Rosicrucian believes that which he knows.*

He believes in the immutability of eternal law, and that every cause has a certain effect. He knows that the truth cannot lie, and that the promises made to him by the king will be fulfilled, if he does not himself hinder their fulfilment. He is, therefore, inaccessible to doubt or fear, and puts implicit confidence in the divine principle of truth, which has become alive and conscious within his heart.

14. *The Rosicrucian's hope is firm.*

Spiritual hope is the certain conviction resulting from a knowledge of the law, that the truths recognised by faith will grow and be fulfilled; it is the knowledge of the heart, and very different from the intellectual speculation of the reasoning brain. His faith rests upon the rock of direct perception and cannot be overthrown. He knows that in everything, however evil it may appear to be, there is a germ of good, and he hopes that in the course of evolution that germ will become developed, and thus evil be transformed into good.

15. *The Rosicrucian cannot be vanquished by suffering.*

He knows that there is no light without shadow, no evil without some good, and that strength only grows by resistance. Having once recognised the existence of the Divine principle within everything, external changes are to him of little importance, and do not deserve great attention. His main object is to hold on to his spiritual possessions, and not to lose the crown which he has gained in the battle of life.

16. *The Rosicrucian will adways remain a member of his society.*

Names are of little importance. The principle which presides over the Rosicrucian Society is the truth; and he who knows the truth, and follows it in practice, is a member of the society over which the truth practises. If all names were changed and all languages altered, the truth would remain the same; and he who lives in the truth will live even if all nations should pass away.

These are the sixteen signs of the true Rosicrucians; which have been revealed to a pilgrim by an angel who took away the heart of the pilgrim, leaving in its place a fiery coal, which is now incessantly burning and glowing with love of the universal brotherhood of humanity.

ROSICRUCIAN JEWELS.

The most valuable jewel of the Rosicrucians is WISDOM, which is represented by a pure DIAMOND in the centre of the ROSE, but the CROSS is adorned with twelve jewels of priceless value, in all of which the power that resides in the truth is manifested. These jewels are:

1. *Jasper* (dark green). The power of active light, multiplying itself to a sevenfold degree, and evolving seven states of the one light, by which the seven states of darkness may be consumed.

2. *Hyacinth* (yellow). LOVE, born from the matrix of Light, manifesting itself as it grows, and emitting red rays. Its power overcomes the spirit of anger and violence.

3. *Chrysolite* (white). Princely wisdom. It confounds that which is foolish and vain, subdues it, and comes out of the battle victorious.

4. *Sapphire* (blue). Truth; originating and growing out of its own essence. It overcomes doubt and vacillation.

5. *Smaragd* (green). The blooming spring in its eternal justice, destroying the unjust attributes of a perverted and degenerate nature, and opening the fountain of infinite treasures.

6. *Topaz* (golden). The symbol of peace, mild and pleasant. It suffers no impurity or division to exist, neither does it admit that which causes separation and quarrels. It heals ruptures and cures wounds.

7. *Amethyst* (violet). Impartiality, equilibrium of justice and judgment. It cannot be falsified, bent, or counterfeited. It weighs all things in the scales of justice, and is opposed to fraud, cruelty, or tyranny.

8. *Beryl* (diverse colours). Meekness, humility; the equal temperature of the spirit, being kind and good, and overcoming wrath, stubbornness, and bitterness.

9. *Sardis* (light red). The high magical FAITH, growing into power, and destroying fear, scepticism, and superstition.

10. *Chrysoprase* (light green). Invisible power and strength, overcoming all opposition, allowing nothing to remain which could possibly resist the law.

11. *Sardonyx* (striped). Triumphant JOY and gladness, flowing from the eternal fountain of happiness, destroying all sorrow and sadness. (May it bless you!).

12. *Chalcedony* (striped). The crown of Victory, dominion, glory. The keystone and the greatest of all miracles, turning everything to the glorification of GOD.

ROSICRUCIAN SYMBOLS

SIGNS FROM THE HEART OF THE CELESTIAL MOTHER.

(From the work of Antonio Ginther. August Vindelicorum. 1741.)

Prænesis. A ship in the open sea, with a floating anchor, and a star shining overhead, with the inscription: *Hac monstrante viam.*

Emblema 1. An open book with the name MARIA, and a heart transfixed by a sword, with the inscription: *Omnibus in omnibus.*

2. A seven-headed monster threatened with a club. Inscription: *In virtute tua.*

3. A closed and sealed door with an angel attempting to open it. Inscription: *Signatur ne perdatur.*

4. A landscape representing an island. The sun rises and the stars shine. Inscription: *Aurora ab lacrymis.*

5. An orange tree bearing fruits, of which the inner part is sweet, while the rind is bitter. Inscription: *Dulce amarum.*

6. An altar with a fire upon it, in which a heart is burning, sending out a sweet odour. Inscription: *In odorem suavitatis.*

7. A pure white lily in a flower-pot, standing in a garden. Inscription: *Virginei laus prima pudoris.*

8. An angel separating wheat from chaff by means of a sieve. Inscription: *Dimittit inanes.*

9. A ring with a jewel exhibited upon a table. Inscription: *Honori invincem.*

10. A globe illuminated by the full moon. Inscription: *Plena sibi et aliis.*

11. Jacob's ladder with seven steps, reaching from the earth up to heaven. Inscription: *Descendendo ascendendo.*

12. A sun-dial attached to the wall of a tower. Inscription: *Altissimus obnumbrat.*

13. The signs of the Zodiac, with the sun passing through the sign of the Virgin. Inscription: *Jam mitius ardet.*

14. A hen brooding in a stable, brooding over eggs. Inscription: *Parit in alieno.*

15. Two palm-trees, inclined towards each other. Inscription: *Blando se pace salutant.*

16. A grape-vine, cut from the trunk, is weeping. Inscription: *Ut gaudeas mero.*

17. A plant, representing a myrrh. Inscription: *Amara sed salubris.*

18. A painter's easel, with a cloth ready for painting. Inscription: *Qua forma placebit.*

19. A heart transfixed by a sword. Inscription: *Usque ad divisionem animæ.*
20. Two doves pecking at each other. Inscription: *Amat et castigat.*
21. A passion flower. Inscription: *Delectat et cruciat.*
22. Wolves and sheep, eagles and bats, basking together in the sunshine. Inscription: *Non possentibus offert.*
23. A bird, sitting between thorns and thistles. Inscription: *His ego sustentor.*
24. Ivy winding around a dead tree. Inscription: *Nec mors separavit.*
25. Two hearts in a winepress. Inscription: *Cogit in unum.*
26. A crocodile shedding tears while eating a man. Inscription: *Plorat et devorat.*
27. Wolf devouring a sheep. Inscription: *Non est qui redimat.*
28. Tulips inclining toward the rising sun. Inscription: *Languexit in umbra.*
29. Two stringed musical instruments; a hand plays upon one. Inscription: *Unam tetigis se sat est.*
30. A white lily growing between thorns. Inscription: *Transfixum suavius.*
31. The prophet Jonah thrown into the raging sea. Inscription: *Merger ne mergantur.*
32. The setting sun and the evening star. Inscription: *Sequitur deserta cadentem.*
33. A cross with a snake wound around it. Inscription: *Pharmacum non venenum.*
34. Eagle, rising towards the sun. Inscription: *Ad te levavi oculos.*
35. A squirrel standing upon a log, floating in the water and rowing. Inscription: *Ne merger.*
36. Light tower, illuminating the ocean. Inscription: *Erantibus una micat.*
37. Rock standing in a stormy sea. Inscription: *Non commovebitur.*
38. A diamond exposed upon a table. Inscription: *In puritate pretium.*
39. Grafting a tree. Inscription: *Accipit in sua.*
40. A man hanging upon a tree. Inscription: *Non est hac tutior umbra.*
41. A flock of sheep, each one bearing the letter T upon the forehead. Inscription: *Non habet redargutionem.*
42. Chandelier with seven lights. Inscription: *Non extinguetur.*
43. A solar eclipse. Inscription: *Morientis sideris umbra.*
44. The setting sun and a rainbow shedding tears. Inscription: *Desinit in lacrymas.*
45. Cypress blown at by winds coming from the four quarters of the world. Inscription: *Concussio firmat.*
46. Two hearts surrounded by thorns, with nails and a dagger. Inscription: *Vulneratum vulnerat.*

47. A heart transfixed by a sword and instruments of torture. Inscription: *Superminet omnes.*

48. Beehive, and bees flying around flowers. Inscription: *Currit in odorem.*

49. A chemical furnace with retorts, from which drops are falling. Inscription: *Color elicit imbres.*

50. A man sowing grain into furrows. Inscription: *Ut surgat in ortum.*

51. A cloth spread upon a field and sprinkled with water. Inscription: *A lacrymis candor.*

52. Ocean waves and a bird flying through the furrows of water. Inscription: *Mersa non mergitur.*

53. Noah's dove with an olive branch. Inscription: *Emergere nuntiat orbem.*

54. Flying eagle carrying a lamb. Inscription: *Tulit prædeam tartari.*

55. Rain descending upon flowers. Inscription: *Dulce refrigerium.*

56. Plumb-line and level. Inscription: *Recta a recto.*

57. A hot iron upon an anvil. Inscription: *Dum calet.*

58. Solitary bird sitting in a cave. Inscription: *Gemit dilectum suum.*

59. Elephant drinking blood flowing from a grape. Inscription: *Acuitur in prælium.*

60. Bird escaping from a nest. Inscription: *Ad sidera sursum.*

61. Sunrise rays shining into a heart of adamant. Inscription: *Intima lustrat.*

62. A flying bird attached to a string. Inscription: *Cupio dissolvi.*

63. Two birds of Paradise flying upwards. Inscription: *Innixa ascendit.*

64. A triple crown made of silver, iron, and gold. Inscription: *Curso completo.*

65. The statue of Dagon thrown down and broken to pieces. A corpse. Inscription: *Cui honorem honorem.*

66. The Red Sea dividing for the passage of the Israelites. Inscription: *Illue iter quo ostendum.*

67. Labyrinth with a human figure therein. A hand extended from heaven holds a thread reaching down to the figure. Inscription: *Hac duce tuta via est.*

68. A camp. Among the tents is a standard bearing the image of a man. Inscription: *Præsidium et decus.*

69. A clock, whose finger points to the second hour. Inscription: *Ultima secunda.*

70. Ship at sea carrying a light. Fishes and birds are attracted by the glow. Inscription: *Veniunt ad lucem.*

Epilogus.—Noah's ark in tranquil water. Inscription: *Non mergitur, sed extollitur.*

SIGNS REFERRING TO THE DIVINE CHILD.

(From the above-mentioned work.)

Prænesis.—A hen with chickens under her wings. A hawk preying in the air above. Inscription: *Sub umbra alarum tuarum.*

Emblema. 1. A figure kneeling and holding a book wherein is represented a fiery heart. Inscription: *Tolle lege.*

2. Altar upon which a fire is lighted by a sunray. Inscription: *Extinctos suscitat ignes.*

3. Sunray falling through a lens and setting a ship on fire. Inscription: *Ignis ab Primo.*

4. Sun shining upon a lambskin extended upon the earth. Inscription: *Descendit de cæis.*

5. A chrysalis upon a leaf. Inscription: *Ecce venio.*

7. The sea and the rising sun. Inscription: *Renovabit faciem terræ.*

8. A rising sun eclipsed by the moon. Inscription: *Condor ut exorior.*

9. A chicken and an eagle in the air. The former is protected against the latter by a shield. Inscription: *A facie persequentis.*

10. A rose in the midst of a garden. Inscription: *Hæc mihi sola placet.*

11. A lamb burning upon an altar. Inscription: *Deus non despicies.*

12. Dogs hunting. Inscription: *Fuga salutem.*

13. A lamb dying at the foot of a cross. Inscription: *Obediens usque ad mortem.*

14. The ark of the covenant. Rays of lightning. Inscription: *Procul este profani.*

15. Sun in the midst of clouds. Inscription: *Fulgura in pluvium fuit.*

16. Sun shining upon sheep and wolves. Inscription: *Super robos et malos.*

17. A well and a pitcher. Inscription: *Hauriar, non exhauriar.*

18. Animals entering the ark. Inscription: *Una salutem.*

19. Shepherd carrying a lamb. Inscription: *Onus meum leve.*

20. Sheep drinking at a well. The water is stirred by a pole. Inscription: *Similem dant vulnera formam.*

21. A dove sitting upon a globe. Inscription: *Non sufficit una.*

22. Light penetrating the clouds. Inscription: *Umbram fugat veritas.*

23. A vineyard and the rising sun. Inscription: *Pertransiit beneficiendo.*

24. Three hearts with a sieve floating above them. Inscription: *Cælo contrito resurgent.*

25. Swan cleaning his feathers before proceeding to eat. Inscription: *Antequam comedum.*

26. A hungry dog howling at the moon. Inscription: *Inanis impetus.*

27. Ark of the covenant drawn by two oxen. Inscription: *Sancta sancte.*

28. A winepress. Inscription: *Premitur ut experimat.*

29. An opening bud. Inscription: *Vulneribus profundit opes.*

30. Amor shooting arrows at a heart. Inscription: *Donec attingam.*

31. Cross and paraphernalia for crucifixion. Inscription: *Præbet non prohibet.*

32. A sunflower looking towards the rising sun. Inscription: *Usque ad occasum.*

33. Drops of sweat falling down in a garden. Inscription: *Tandem resoluta venit.*

34. Sword protruding from the clouds. Inscription: *Cædo noncedo.*

35. Hammer and anvil, a forge and a fire. Inscription: *Ferendo, non feriendo.*

36. A ram crowned with thorns upon an altar. Inscription: *Victima coronata.*

37. A sheep carrying animals. Inscription: *Quam grave portat onus.*

38. A crucified person and a snake upon a tree. Inscription: *Unde mors unde vita.*

39. A tree shedding tears into three dishes. Inscription: *Et læsa medelam.*

40. A spring fountain. Inscription: *Rigat ut erigat.*

41. A heart offered to an eagle. Inscription: *Redibit ad Dominum.*

42. A heart upon a cross surrounded by thorns, crowned with a laurel. Inscription: *Pignus amabile pacis.*

43. Bird persecuted by a hawk seeks refuge in the cleft of a rock. Inscription: *Hoc tuta sua sub antro.*

44. Target with a burning heart in the centre; Amor shooting arrows at it. Inscription: *Trahe mi post te.*

45. Pelican feeding her young ones with her own blood. Inscription: *Ut vitam habeant.*

47. Phœnix sinking into the flames. Inscription: *Hic mihi dulce mori.*

48. Blood from a lamb flowing into a cup. Inscription: *Purgantes temperat ignis.*

49. Clouds from which proceed rays of lightning. Inscription: *Lux recto fatumque noscenti.*

50. Eagle flying towards the sun. Inscription: *Tunc facie ad faciem.*

Epilogus.—A hedgehog, having rolled in fruits, is covered with them. Inscription: *Venturi providus ævi.*

He who can see the meaning of all these allegories has his eyes open.

TABULA SMARAGDINA.

`ERBA SECRETORUM HERMETIS.

It is, beyond any doubt, most certain and true, that the Below is like the Above, and thereby can be accomplished the miracle of one only thing. As all things are derived from only one thing, by the will and the word of the One who created it in his mind; likewise all things result from this unity by the order of nature. Its father is the sun, its mother the moon; the air carries it in its womb; its nurse is the earth. This thing is the origin of all perfections that exist throughout the world. Its power is most perfect when it has again been reduced to earth.

Separate the earth from the fire, and the subtle from that which is gross; act with prudence, understanding, and modesty. It rises up from the earth to the heavens, and returns again to the earth, taking unto itself the power of the Above and the Below. Thus you will obtain the glory of the whole world. Therefore discard all ignorance and impotency. This is the strongest of all powers, for it overcomes all subtle things, and can penetrate through all that is gross. Thus was the world created, and from this originate rare combinations, and are wrought miracles of various kinds. Therefore have I been called Hermes Trismegistus, having obtained thee-parts of the wisdom of the whole world. This is what is to be said about the masterwork of the alchymical art.

Chapter Eight.

ALCHEMY.

Quæ sunt in superis hac inferioribus insunt; Quod monstrat coelum, id terra frequenter habet. Ignis, Aqua et Fluitans, due sunt contraria; Felix talia si jungis, sit tibi scire satis.

ALCHEMY is that science which results from a knowledge of God, Nature, and Man. A perfect knowledge of either of them cannot be obtained without the knowledge of the other two, for these three are one and inseparable. Alchemy is not merely an intellectual, but a spiritual science; because that which belongs to the spirit can only be spiritually known. Nevertheless, it is a science dealing with material things, for spirit and matter are only two opposite manifestations or "poles" of the eternal one. Alchemy is an art, and as every art requires an artist to exercise it, likewise this divine science and art can be practised only by those who are in possession of the divine power necessary for that purpose. It is true that the external manipulations required for the production of certain alchemical preparations may, like an ordinary chemical process, be taught to anybody capable of reasoning; but the results which he would accomplish would be without life, for only he in whom the true life has awakened can awaken it from its sleep in the *prima materia*, and cause visible forms to grow from the *Chaos* of nature.

Alchemy in its highest aspects deals with the spiritual regeneration of man, and teaches how a god may be made out of a human being or, to express it more correctly, how to establish the conditions necessary for the development of divine powers in man, so that a human being may become a god by the power of God, in the same sense as a seed becomes a plant by the aid of the four elements, and the action of the invisible fifth. Alchemy in its more material aspect teaches how minerals, metals, plants, and animals, and men, may be generated, or made to grow from their "seeds"; or, in other words, how that generation, which is accomplished during long periods of time in the due course of the action of natural laws, may be accomplished in a comparatively very short time, if these natural laws are guided and supplied with material, by the spiritual knowledge of man. There is no doubt in my mind that gold can be made to grow by alchemical means; but it requires an Alchemist to make the experiment succeed, and he who is attracted by the power of gold will not obtain possession of the spiritual power necessary to practise that art.

It is not the object of these pages to furnish proof to the sceptic that Alchemy is a truth, nor to furnish arguments on the strength of which the incredulous may become persuaded to believe in its possibility. To believe in a thing of which one has no knowledge would be of little benefit; but those who have some spiritual knowledge of Alchemy, perhaps having studied it in some former incarnation, may receive some benefit from a perusal of this chapter, as it may serve to bring that which they already spiritually know to the understanding of their mind.*

It is a mistake to confound Alchemy with Chemistry. Modern Chemistry is a science which deals merely with the external forms in which the element of matter is manifesting itself. It never produces anything new. We may mix and compound and decompose two or more chemical bodies an unlimited number of times, and cause them to appear under various different forms, but at the end we will have no augmentation of substance, nor anything more than the combinations of the substances that have been employed at the beginning. Alchemy does not mix or compound anything, it causes that which already exists in a latent state to become active and grow. Alchemy is, therefore, more comparable to botany or agriculture than to Chemistry; and, in fact, the growth of a plant, a tree, or an animal is an alchemical process going on in the alchemical laboratory of nature, and performed by the great Alchemist, the power of God acting in nature.

The nature of Alchemy is clearly explained by Johannes Tritheim, who says:—

"God is an essential and hidden fire in all things, and especially in man. That fire generates all things. It has generated them, and will generate them in the future, and that which is generated is the true divine light in all eternity. God is a fire; but no fire can burn, and no light appear within nature without the addition of air to cause the combustion, and likewise the Holy Spirit in you must act as a divine 'air' or breath, coming out of the divine fire and breathing upon the fire within the soul, so that the light will appear, for the light must be nourished by the fire, and this light is love and gladness and joy within the eternal deity. This light is *Jesus*, having emanated from eternity from *Jehovah*. He who has this light not within himself is in the fire without light; but if the light is in him, then is the *Christ* in him, and takes form in him, and such a person will know that light as it exists in nature.

"All things such as we see are in their interior fire and light, wherein is hidden the essence of the spirit. All things are a trinity of fire, light, and air. In other words, '*Spirit*,' the 'father,' is a divine superessential light; the 'son,' the light having become manifest; the 'holy spirit' a divine superessential air and motion. The fire resides within the heart and sends its rays through the whole body of man, causing it to live;

---

* There are two kinds of knowledge in man, namely, that which belongs to his spirit *(Budhi)*, and that which belongs to his mind *(Manas)*. The former is, so to say, the quintessence of what man has learned in previous incarnations; the latter is that which he has learned in his present life. If he were to succeed to rise up in his mind to the sphere of his spirit, to unite his Budhi with his Manas; then would the mind share the knowledge which the spirit possesses.

but no light is born from the fire without the presence of the spirit of holiness."

To express this in other words we may say—All things are made of *thought*, and exist in the universal mind (the *astral light*), and within each is latent the *will*, by whose action they may become developed and their powers unfolded. This takes place under favourable circumstances by the slow and unconscious action of the universal will acting in nature, and may be accomplished in a very short time by the aid of the conscious will of the alchemist; but before the will of a person can accomplish such wonders in external substances, his will must first become self-conscious within itself; the light that shines from the centre of his own heart, must become living and bright before it can act upon those substances with which the Alchemist deals. He in whom this divine light of the Christ (the *Atma*) has not awakened to life, is virtually asleep in the spirit, and can act upon spiritual things no more than a man can deal with material substances while he sleeps; but this fact will hardly be acknowledged or comprehended by the superficial scientist and rationalist, who imagine themselves to be fully awake, and therefore the secrets of alchemy are an inexplicable mystery to them, which can be disposed of in no other way than by being denied or laughed away. Alchemy was known at the most ancient times. It was no secret to the initiates among the ancient Brahmins and the Egyptians; and the Bible, if read in the light of the *Cabala*, will be found to be the description of an alchemical process. The *Aleph* א represent three fiery flames, nevertheless, it is only one letter. In Magic it means *AOH*, the Father, the one from which all the rest take their origin, the *Alpha* and likewise the *Omega*, the beginning and also the end. As the air causes the fire to burn and to emit a light, likewise the Holy Spirit (without whose presence nothing can be accomplished) nourishing the divine fire with the soul, causes the living light of the Christ to become manifest. This is also indicated in the three first letters of the word פדאשיח, for the פ means "Ben," the son; the א *AOH*, the father; and ד means "Ruach," or spirit. This, then, is a trinity of father, son, and spirit, and its quality is indicated by the following syllable שיח, indicating the true generation, for the ש is the letter symbolizing the fire, and the י the light. The pronounciation of the former is like the hissing of the flame, but the latter issues mildly from the fire, as it is likewise born mildly and humbly within the human soul while the כ symbolizes the spirit and the power of the outspoken word.

The "*Song of Solomon*," in the *Old Testament*, is a description of the processes of alchemy. In this *Song* the *Subjectum* is described in *Cant. i.*, 5; the *Lilium artis* in *C. ii.*, 1; the *Preparation* and *Purification* in *C. ii.*, 4; the *Fire* in *C. ii.*, 7, and *C. iv.*, 16; the *Putrefaction* in *C. iii.*, 1; *Sublimation* and *Distillation* in *C. iii.*, 6; *Coagulation* and *Change of Colours*, *C. v.*, 9 to 14; *Fixation*, *C. ii*, 12, and *C viii*, 4;

Multiplication, C. vi., 7; *Augmentation* and *Projection, C. viii.* 8, etc., etc.

With all this it must not be supposed that the practice of Alchemy consists merely in the exercise of the will and the imagination, or that the products obtained are merely imaginary and intangible or invisible to mortal eyes. On the contrary, no alchemical processes can be accomplished without the presence of visible and tangible matter, as it is so to say a spiritualizing of "matter." There is no transformation of "matter" into "spirit," as some people believe, for each of the seven principles of eternal nature is unchangeable, and remains for ever in its own centre, in the same sense as darkness cannot be turned into light, although a light may be kindled within the darkness, in consequence of which the darkness will disappear. Likewise within each material form there sleeps the divine spirit, the light, which may become awakened to life and activity, and illuminate the body and cause it to live and to grow. Of the qualities of the powers of that light, or even of its existence, modern chemistry has no knowledge and no names to describe it; but they are described under various names in the Bible, and in the still older religious books of the East.

There is a visible substance and an invisible one; a tangible water and one that is beyond the reach of perception by the physical senses; a visible fire and an invisible magic fire; neither can either of these accomplish anything without the other, for in the practice of Alchemy, as in the regeneration of man, that which is above must be made to penetrate that which is below, so that the lower may enter into a higher state of existence.

THE "PRIMA MATERIA."

If we wish to know nature we must learn to know God, and God cannot be known without a knowledge of one's own divine self. The spiritual substance of which external visible nature is an imperfect expression and manifestation, has been called *"Prima Materia"*; it is the material for the formation of a new heaven and a new earth. It is like "water," or a "crystalline ocean," if compared with our grossly material earth, it is at once fire, water, air, and earth, corporeal in its essence, and nevertheless, incorporeal relatively to our physical forms.

In it as the *"Chaos,"* are contained the germs, or seeds, or "potencies" of all things that ever existed, and of all that ever will exist in the future. It is the soul, or *corpus* of nature, and by means of the *magic fire*, it may be extricated from all substances, and be rendered corporeal and visible. It is a unity, and nevertheless a trinity, according to its aspects as *Sulphur, Mercury,* and *Salt*. These three are distinct qualities characterising the spirit of light, and nevertheless they are nothing different from the essence of the light, and this light is eternal nature, or the soul of the world.

This *primordial matter* contains the powers that go to form minerals and metals, vegetables and animals, and everything that breathes; all forms are hidden within its depths, and it is therefore, the true principium or beginning of all things. It is the play and battle ground for all the astral influences that come from the stars and the birthplace of the beings that inhabit the astral plane, not less than of those that are born into the (to us) visible world. It is the womb of eternal nature from which everything that exists is born by the power of the spirit acting within. From its fertile soil are produced good and evil fruits, wholesome and noxious plants, harmless and poisonous animals, for God is no distinguisher of persons, or favouring any particular individual; each receives its share of life, and will, according to its capacity to receive, and each becomes ultimately that which its character destines it to be.

THE "SPIRITUS UNIVERSALIS,"
Without which no alchemical experiment will succeed.

Johannes Tritheim, an abbott and alchemist, whose writings are plainer and more comprehensible than any other alchemical book, says:—

All things have been made by the power of the divine word, which is the divine spirit or breath that emanated from the divine fountain in the beginning. This breath is the spirit or soul of the world, and is called the "*spiritus mundi.*" It was at first like air, and contracted into a fog or nebular substance, and afterwards became "water" (*Akasa*). This "water" was at first all spirit and life, because it was permeated by and made alive by the spirit. It was dark in the depths; but through the outspoken word the light became generated therein, and then the darkness was illumined by the light, and the "soul of the world" (the *astral light*) had its beginning. This spiritual light, which we call "Nature," or the soul of the world, is a spiritual body, which, by means of Alchemy, can be made tangible and visible; but as it exists in an invisible state, therefore is it called "spirit."

"This is an universal and living fluid diffused throughout the All of Nature, and which pervades all beings. It is the most subtle of all substances, the most powerful on account of its inherent qualities, penetrating all bodies, and causing the forms in which it is active to live. By its action it frees the forms of all imperfections, and renders the impure pure, the imperfect perfect, and causes that which is mortal to become immortal by becoming fixed therein."

"This essence of spirit has emanated from the centre in the beginning, and is incorporated into the substance of which the world is formed. It is the *Salt of the Earth*, and without its presence the grass would not grow, nor the fields be green; and the more this essence is condensed, concentrated, and coagulated in the forms, the more enduring will they become. This substance is the most subtle of all things, incorruptible, unchangeable in its essence, pervading the infinity of space. The sun and the planets are merely condensed states of this universal principle, and they distribute their abundance from their throbbing hearts, and send them into the forms of the lower worlds and into all beings, acting through their own centres, and leading the forms higher up on the road to perfection. The forms in which this living principle becomes fixed become perfect and permanent, so that they will neither rust nor decay, nor be changed on being exposed to the air; neither can such forms be dissolved by water, nor be destroyed by fire, nor eaten up by the elements of the earth.

"This spirit can be obtained in the same manner in which it is communicated to the earth by the stars; and this takes place by means of water, which serves as its vehicle. It is not the *Philosopher's Stone*, but the latter may be prepared of it by causing that which is volatile to become fixed.

"I admonish you to pay strict attention to the boiling of the water, and not to allow your minds to be disturbed by things of minor importance. Boil it slowly, and let it putrefy until it attains the proper colour, for in the water of Life is contained the germ of wisdom. By the art of boiling the water will become transformed into earth. This earth is to be changed into a pure crystalline fluid, from which an excellent red fire is produced; but this water and fire, grown together into one essence, produces the great *Panacea*, composed of meekness and strength: the *lamb* and the *lion* in one."

THE SECRET FIRE.

In H. P. Blavatsky's book *"The Voice of the Silence,"* the secret fire of the Alchemists is described as *"Kundalini,"* the "serpentine," or annular working power in the body of the ascetic. "It is an electric fiery occult or *Fohatic* power, the great pristine force which underlies all organic and inorganic matter"; and in another place the author says: "It is an electro-spiritual force, a creative power which, when aroused into action, can as easily kill as it can create."

This point is the reason why the secrets of Alchemy are not divulged to the curious, and why only those who have gained the power to control their own self will be told how that power can be aroused in man.

In regard to this "secret fire," the Rosicrucians say:

The potentialities in nature are aroused by the action of the secret fire, assisted by the elementary fire. The secret fire is invisible, and is contained within all things. It is the most potential and powerful fire, with which the external visible fire cannot be compared. It is the fire with which Moses burned the golden calf, and that which Jeremiah hid away, and which seventy years after was found by the knowing ones, but which, by that time had become a thick water. (2 *Maccab.* I. and II.)

Without the possession of this magic fire, no alchemical process can be accomplished, and therefore it is recommended in the "Secret Symbols of the Rosicrucians," that the student of Alchemy should above all seek for the fire.

THE FOUR ALCHEMICAL RULES.

1. Follow Nature.

It is useless to seek for the sun by the light of a candle.

2. First know; then act.

Real knowledge exists in the triangle composed of *seeing, feeling,* and *understanding.*

3. Use no vulgar processes. Use only one vessel, one fire, one instrument.

The door to success lies in the unity of will and purpose and the proper adaptation of the means to the end. There are many roads leading to the celestial centre. He who follows the chosen path may succeed, while he who atempts to walk on many paths will be delayed.

4. Keep the fire constantly burning.

If the molten metals are allowed to cool off before they are transformed into higher ones, they will become hard again, and the whole process will have to be recommenced from the beginning. Use the inextinguishable lamp. Its light will not go out unless it is driven away by force.

THE FIVE THINGS NECESSARY TO OBSERVE IN THE PRACTICE OF ALCHEMY.

1. To recognize the true PRIMA MATERIA.

It is to be found everywhere; but if you do not find it in your own house, you will find it nowhere. It is a living substance that can be discovered only in places inhabited by man. It is the only substance from which the *Philosopher's Stone* can be prepared, and without that substance no genuine silver or gold can be made. In thirty pounds of ordinary mercury, there is usually not more than one pound of the true substance; and a hundred pounds of ordinary sulphur usually contain not more than one pound of that which is useful. It can only be found above the earth, but not below it. It is before everybody's eyes; no one can live without it; everybody uses it; the poor usually possess more of it than the rich; the ignorant esteem it highly, but the learned ones often throw it away. The children play with it in the street, and yet it is invisible. It can be perceived by the sense of feeling, but it cannot be seen with the material eye.

2. Use for the preparation of the PRIMA MATERIA *only the rose-coloured blood of the Red Lion and the pure white gluten of the Eagle.*

Let your Will be strong, but without anger, and your Thoughts be pure from that which infects the lower strata of the earth's atmosphere. Let the fire of the divine Will penetrate deeply within your soul, and elevate your mind to the highest regions of thought.

3. Obtain the sacred Fire.

It is not of man's making; it cannot be bought, but it is given for nothing to those who deserve it.

4. Then follow Multiplication and Increase, for which purpose weight and measure are necessary.

Weigh all things with the scales of justice, and measure them by the rule of reason.

5. *The fifth is the Application, that is to say the Projection upon the metals.*

This will be accomplished by nature without artificial aid.

AXIOMATA HERMETICA.

1. *Whatever may be accomplished by a simple method should not be attempted by a complicated one.*

There is only one Truth, whose existence requires no proof, because it is itself proof enough to those who are capable of perceiving it. Why should we enter into complexness to seek for that which is simple? The sages say: "*Ignis et Azoth tibi sufficiunt.*" The body is already in your possession. All that you require is the fire and the air.

2. *No substance can be made perfect without long suffering.*

Great is the error of those who imagine that the *Philosopher's Stone* can be hardened without being first dissolved; their time and labour is wasted.

3. *Nature must be aided by art whenever she is deficient in power.*

Art may be the handmaid of nature, but cannot supplant her mistress. Art without nature is always unnatural. Nature without art is not always perfect.

4. *Nature cannot be amended except in her own self.*

The nature of a tree cannot be changed by trimming the branches or by the addition of ornaments; it can be improved only by improving the soil upon which it grows, or by grafting.

5. *Nature enjoys, comprehends, and overcomes nature.*

There is no other actual knowledge than the knowledge of self. Every being can only truly realize its own existence, but not that of any element entirely foreign to it.

6. *He who does not know motion does not know nature.*

Nature is the product of emotion. At the moment in which eternal motion should cease, all nature would cease to exist. He who does not know the motions that are taking place in his body is a stranger in his own house.

7. *Whatever produces the same effect as is produced by a compound is similar to the latter.*

The One is greater than all the rest of the numbers, for from it an infinite variety of mathematical magnitudes may be evolved, but no change is possible without the all-pervading presence of the One, whose qualities are manifest in its manifestations.

8. *No one can pass from one extreme to another except through a medium.*

An animal cannot become divine before it becomes human. That which is unnatural must become natural before its nature can become spiritual.

9. *Metals cannot be changed into other metals without having been first reduced to prima materia.*

The self-will, opposed to the divine, must cease before the divine Will can enter into the heart. We must become unsophisticated, like children; before the word of wisdom can speak in our mind.

10. *The unripe must be assisted by the ripe.*

Thus fermentation will be induced. The law of *Induction* rules in all departments of nature.

11. *In the Calcination the Corpus is not reduced, but augmented, in quantity.*

True asceticism consists in giving up that which one does not want after having received something better.

12. *In Alchemy nothing can bear fruit without having first been mortified.*

The light cannot shine through matter unless the matter has become sufficiently refined to allow the passage of the rays.

13. *That which kills produces life; that which causes death causes resurrection; that which destroys creates.*

Nothing comes out of nothing. The creation of a new form is conditioned by the destruction (transformation) of the old one.

14. *Everything containing a seed may be augmented, but not without the assistance of nature.*

It is only through the seed that the fruit bearing more seeds comes into existence.

15. *Each thing is multiplied and augmented by means of a male and female principle.*

Matter produces nothing unless penetrated by power. Nature creates nothing unless impregnated by Spirit. Thought remains unproductive unless rendered active by Will.

16. *The virtue of each seed is to unite itself with each thing belonging to its own kingdom.*

Each thing in nature is attracted by its own nature represented in other things. Colours and sounds of a similar nature form harmonious units, substances that are related with each other can be combined, animals of the same genus associate with each other, and spiritual powers unite with their own kindred germs.

17. *A pure womb gives birth to a pure fruit.*

Only in the innermost sanctuary of the soul will the mystery of the spirit be revealed.

18. *Fire and heat can only be produced by motion.*

Stagnation is death. The stone thrown into the water forms progressively radiating circles, which are produced by motion. The soul that cannot be moved cannot be elevated, and becomes petrified.

19. *The whole method is begun and finished by only* ONE *method:* THE BOILING.

The great *Arcanum* is a celestial spirit, descending from the sun, the moon, and the stars, and which is brought into perfection in the saturnine object by continuous boiling until it attains the state of sublimation and power necessary to transform the base metals into gold. This operation is performed by the *hermetic fire*. The separation of the subtle from the gross must be done carefully, adding continually water; for the more earthly the materials are, the more must they be diluted and made to move. Continue this process until the separated soul is reunited with the body.

20. *The entire process is accomplished through nothing else but Water.*

It is the same *Water* over which the Spirit of God moved in the beginning, when darkness was upon the face of the deep.

21. *Each thing comes from and out of that into which it will be resolved again.*

That which is earthy comes from the earth; that which belongs to the stars is obtained from the stars; that which is spiritual comes from the Spirit, and returns to God.

22. *Where the true principles are absent, the results will be imperfect.*

Mere imitations cannot produce genuine results. Merely imaginary love, wisdom, and power can only be effective in the realm of illusions.

23. *Art begins where nature ceases to act.*

Art accomplishes by means of nature that which nature is unable to accomplish if unaided by art.

24. *The hermetic art is not attained by great variety of methods, the* LAPIS *is only one.*

There is only one eternal, unchangeable truth. It may appear under many different aspects; but in that case it is not the truth that changes: it is we who change our modes of conceiving of it.

25. *The substance of which the* ARCANUM *is prepared should be pure, indestructible, and incombustible.*

It should be pure of grossly material elements, indestructible by doubt, and incapable of being burned up in the fire of passion.

26. *Do not seek for the seed of the* PHILOSOPHER'S STONE *in the Elements.*

Only at the Centre of the fruit is that seed to be found.

27. *The substance of the Philosopher's Stone is mercurial.*

Those that are wise are seeking for it in the mercury; the fool seeks to create it out of his own empty brain.

28. *The seed of the metals is in the metals, and the metals are born of themselves.*

The growth of the metals is very slow; but it may be hastened by the addition of Patience.

29. *Use only perfect metals.*

Crude mercury, such as is usually found in European countries, is perfectly useless for this work. Worldly wisdom is foolishness in the eyes of the Lord.

30. *That which is hard and thick must be made subtle and thin by calcination.*

This is a very painful and tedious process, because it is necessary to remove even the root of evil, and this causes the heart to bleed, and tortured nature to cry out.

31. *The foundation of this art is to reduce the* CORPORA *into* ARGENTUM VIVUM.

This is the *Solutio Sulphuris Sapientium in Mercurio.* A science without life is a dead science; an intellect without spirituality is only a false and borrowed light.

32. *In the solution the solvent and the dissolved must remain together.*

Fire and water must be made to combine. Thought and love must remain for ever united.

33. *If the seed is not treated by warmth and moisture, it will be useless.*

Coldness contracts and dryness hardens the heart, but the fire of divine love expands it, and the water of thought dissolves the residua.

34. *The earth produces no fruit unless moistened repeatedly.*

No revelation takes place in the darkness except through the light.

35. *The moistening takes place by water, with which it has the closest affinity.*

The body itself is a product of thought, and has therefore the closest affinity with the mind.

36. *Everything dry naturally tends to attract the moisture which it requires to become complete in its constitution.*

The One, from which all things are produced, is perfect; and therefore all things contain within themselves the tendency and possibility for perfection.

37. *A seed is useless and impotent unless it is put in its appropriate matrix.*

A soul cannot develop and progress without an appropriate body, because it is the physical body that furnishes the material for its development.

38. *Active heat produces in that which is moist blackness; in that which is dry, whiteness; and in that which is white, a yellow colour.*

First comes mortification, then calcination, and afterwards the golden glow produced by the light of the sacred fire illuminating the purified soul.

39. *The fire must be moderate, uninterrupted, slow, equal, moist, warm, white, light, all-embracing, enclosed, penetrating, living, inexhaustible, and the one used by nature.*

It is the fire that descends from heaven to bless all mankind.

40. *All operations must take place in only one vessel and without removing it from the fire.*

The substance used for the preparation of the *Philosopher's Stone* should be collected only in one place and not be dispersed in many places. If the gold has once lost its brightness, it is difficult to restore it.

41. *The vessel should be well closed, so that the water may not run*

out of it, or the air escape; it ought to be hermetically sealed, because if the spirit were to find a place to escape, the power would be lost; and furthermore it should be well closed, so that nothing foreign and impure can enter and become mixed with it.

There should always be put at the door of the laboratory a sentinel with a flaming sword to examine all visitors, and to reject those that are not worthy to be admitted.

42. Do not open the vessel until the moistening is completed.

If the vessel is prematurely opened, most of the labour is lost.

43. The more the Lapis is nursed and nourished, the more will it increase.

Divine wisdom is inexhaustible; the limitation exists only in the capacity of the form to receive it.

THE END.

The following mystical pictures are not related to this book.

They have been included for your enjoyment.

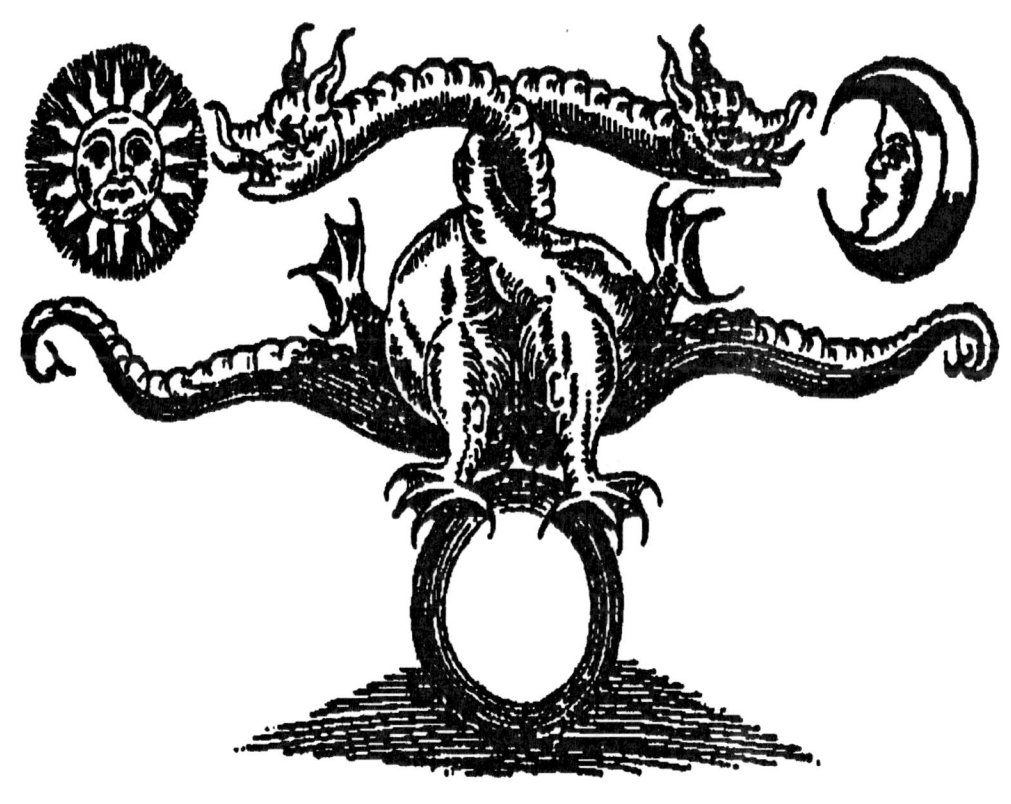

Pictures 1

Pictures 2

Pictures 5

ALCHYMIA
(From Thurneysser's Quinta Essentia, 1570)

Pictures 7

Pictures 8

Pictures 9

Assyrian Type of Gilgamesh

Printed in the United Kingdom
by Lightning Source UK Ltd.
106016UKS00001B/37